Cairo Child

'All gone! Tonight we are historians.
We speak now only of history'
Greek Alexandrian quoted by David Holden.
Egypt. A Traveller's Anthology. Ed. Christopher Pick

Cairo Child

by

Paula Ormerod

Date of Publication:
September 2004

Published by:
Sphinx Press
P.O. Box 170
Wantage, Oxon
OX12 8WQ

Printed by:
ProPrint
Riverside Cottages
Old Great North Road
Stibbington
Peterborough PE8 6LR

ISBN: 0-9547645-0-1

AUTHOR'S NOTE

These memoirs were originally written for my sons to enlighten them about three things: my family history, my life in Cairo during the dying days of the British presence in Egypt and the social mores of the time.

I deliberately did no research apart from checking on a few historical facts and dates, and referring to family papers. I wanted to record my memories, pure and simple. But memories are unreliable and if I have offended or if my memory does not coincide with that of others, I am sorry. I have been as honest as I know how.

Naively, I thought I could leave my feelings and views out of the narrative. Of course that proved impossible and, in the writing, this has also turned out to be the story of a child's struggle to understand the adult world and of her joining that world but without yet achieving maturity.

* * *

I want to thank my family and many friends who have urged me to reach a wider audience, in particular Daphne Rock for her unfailing support; my son Nicholas for editing and proof-reading the final manuscript, his wife Penny for providing the cover illustration and Lynn Truss and Mark Lawson for the guidance and encouragement they offered me at an Arvon Foundation course at a point when I nearly gave up.

P.O. 2004

CONTENTS

PREQUEL

My only claim to fame is that I was one of the first to enter Tutankhamun's tomb after it was opened. This was by virtue of the fact that my mother was part of the press corps at the opening and I was born four months later. It is impossible to overstate the archaeological importance of the discovery of this tomb, nor the sensation it caused at the time. Gerald O'Farrell has described it as 'the greatest show on earth in the 1920s'.

There is a story to be told about this and it solves a Fleet Street mystery. There is no official account of how *The Times* correspondent, who had sole rights to the Tutankhamun tomb 'story', was scooped by the rest of the press. The nearest present day equivalent would be that the news was broken by the newspapers and all the television channels except the BBC.

Here is my mother's version:

My father was part of the press corps. He was at the time Egypt correspondent for several papers and agencies including *The Daily Telegraph* and *The Daily Mail.* (No jet-setting journalists from London then.) There was no television and BBC radio had just burst on to an astonished world. So only about half a dozen men and my mother covered the story. She had been determined not to miss the fun and my father allocated to her the job of covering for *The Chicago Daily Tribune.*

Arthur Merton, *The Times* correspondent, was the only journalist to enter the inner chamber of the tomb with the official party. The inner chamber was to prove finally whose tomb this was. The other journalists kicked their heels outside. An Egyptian official emerged from the tomb to relieve himself behind a rock, one of the press corps joined him, asked a few questions – for example, 'was there a great deal of lapis lazuli?' – and returned to his colleagues with the answer – without a doubt, "Tutankhamun's".

They all immediately leapt on to their donkeys, crossed the Nile by felucca to Luxor and cabled the news to London. The next morning the only paper without the news was the London *Times*.

Also the next day, the rest of the journalists were allowed to visit the tomb – and I went with them.

*'Recollection . . . that fragmented vision of elsewhere
with which each of us lives'*
Penelope Lively. A House Unlocked

EARLY YEARS
1923-1933

Midan Ismailia

I was born in Dublin because my mother had wanted to be near her eldest sister and when, a few weeks later, Aunt Vi saw us off on the twelve-day voyage home to Egypt, she wondered how I would survive the journey, my mother was so neurotically incompetent at handling this new baby.

Well, I did arrive safely in Egypt, probably due to the ministrations of the ship stewardess, and on arrival in Cairo my mother wisely engaged a nanny. She was Syrian, a plump, plain woman with a head of tight curls and a ready chuckle. Most importantly, she was gloriously affectionate. Her devotion to me was absolute and she more than compensated for my mother's shortcomings.

Until I was four my parents, Nanny and I lived high, high above Midan Ismailia, presumably named after the Kedive Ismail, who, it was said, in the nineteenth century had been so extravagant that he had reduced Egypt to such great debt that the British bought up the shares in the Suez Canal in 1875 and Anglo-French control of Egypt's finances was established and saved the country from ruin.

The Midan is now called the Midan al Tahrir (Freedom Square) and will be known to any modern tourist, containing as it does the Nile Hilton Hotel and the Cairo Museum. Our building was at that time a fairly smart block of mansion flats near the centre of Cairo and near my father's office off Sharia Kasr el Nil.

The noise rising from the Midan was constant, day and night. There were fewer cars than nowadays but the drivers that there were leaned on their horns as they negotiated the donkey carts, the horse-drawn *gharries* and the over-laden buses. The trams clattered by, their conductors blowing miniature brass bugles each time they stopped or started. And accompanying the noise from the traffic were other sounds:

wailing Arabic music from the coffee shops, the clashing of cymbals from the lemonade sellers in their colourful mediaeval Ottoman costume, the cries of other vendors, occasionally the chanting of workmen as, in a chain, they hauled on a rope or passed buckets one to another.

The Egypt in which I was to spend my childhood was stable and prosperous, in spite of the existence of appalling poverty and an active Nationalist movement which occasionally erupted into violence. For me it was a happy, safe and colourful place to be.

The British Protectorate had officially ended in 1922, but owing to some provisions in the agreement British influence was still powerful. There was an Egyptian monarchy, a democratic government and civil service, but Britain guaranteed to protect the country in the event of war. The three British services were stationed there and the British held senior positions in the judiciary, education and the civil service and British business interests were strong. At the same time it was a truly cosmopolitan country. Every Mediterranean language could be heard in the city streets. While Egypt's main industries of cotton and tourism were in the hands of the Egyptians and British, the French, Italians, Greeks, Belgians and the Jews were also all involved in the economy of the country.

French influence was still noticeable. The centre of Cairo had been rebuilt by Haussmann in the style of the Paris boulevards, Bulaq Bridge, one of the bridges which linked Gezira Island with the mainland, had been designed by Eiffel of the Paris Tower. The counterparts of many middle class villas could be found in any provincial French town and even the street signs were like the French ones: royal blue plaques with white writing. Egyptian law was based on the Napoleonic Code. Educated Egyptians were all fluent in French and official notices were printed in Arabic and French.

My father must have been at this time at the most affluent (never very rich) and most productive time of his career. Perhaps the most prestigious job he had had was before the 1914-18 war as editor in Fleet Street of a monthly called *Great Britain and the Near East*. After a war spent in the Middle East, he had bought up *The Sphinx,* a slender magazine which catered mainly for the winter visitors to Egypt. He went into partnership with its then owner, Max Fischer, to form the Sphinx Publishing Company.

Before the 1914-18 War Egypt had been a favourite winter resort for the rich and famous. The guest lists for the Egyptian hotels for the 1908-09 season included twenty-four members of European royalty, 184 European aristocrats and several English MPs, including Winston Churchill. Considering the long journey each way to Egypt one has to wonder how affairs of state were attended to.

My father recognised a need in the British community after the war and developed the original society news sheet into a weekly glossy magazine. By degrees he widened its scope to introduce a political leader, arts reviews, sports and women's pages, etc. *The Sphinx* became popular and required reading for every middle class home. It was brought out by my father, a sub-editor, his secretary, Lily, an accountant and a couple of office boys. Also on the premises were the printing works, also owned by the company. Max Fischer brought out *The Egyptian Directory,* a cross between a business directory and a Who's Who in Egypt.

At the same time my father was local correspondent for about half a dozen papers and agencies, including *The Daily Mail* and *The Daily Telegraph.* He covered everything for these and had to send a unique account of each story to each paper. He did this alone apart from an Egyptian "stringer" who fed him news. In addition to his professional work, he was honorary secretary of the British Union, which represented British business interests, a keen Rotarian, whose monthly Bulletin he produced, and an active member of the Caledonian Club.

My mother helped him mainly with the entertaining and socialising that the job entailed. She also wrote a weekly gossip column, "The Epistles of Peggy", in which pseudonyms were often used. It was avidly read.

I realised nothing of this background. The centre of my world was the long, cool flat with my sunny nursery at the far end from the dining and drawing rooms.

We were once joined in the Midan Ismailia flat by Granny Seddall, my maternal grandmother. Separated from her husband, she had become entirely dependant on her three daughters and lived for a while with each one. It was her turn to come to us for a while, before moving on to her second daughter, Aunt Rosie, who also lived in Cairo with her husband, Don Llewellyn, who worked with the Shell Company, and her two children, Peggy and Donald. Then Granny would have gone home to Ireland to join Aunt Vi, her eldest daughter, now widowed and living in Dublin. Granny Seddall must have been in her sixties, but she always dressed in long black with a black velvet ribbon round her neck and a large black hat which hid her lovely thick white hair. She was a sad, fragile figure, very quiet. I don't believe she joined in my parents' social life.

Nanny had almost total care of me in my early years, "quality time" with my parents being restricted to a period each early evening when I joined them in the drawing room for a ginger beer, while they sipped their whiskies. She did not, of course, accompany us on our "home" leaves each summer, so I saw more of them then, although both Beatie and Lena, much older cousins on my father's side, were often called in to help out.

Each morning Nanny would take me to the public gardens on Gezira, the island on the Nile. Sometimes we had breakfast in the gardens: a hard-boiled egg with flat Arab bread, sometimes porridge out of a wide thermos flask, always hot, sweet tea. I played with the other children. All nationalities we were – Egyptian, Maltese, Italian, Greek, French. Somehow we communicated in a common language.

Home for lunch and then the statutory siesta. I would then play in the nursery until it was time to join my parents in the drawing room. Nanny would put me to bed and my mother would hear my prayers.

The nursery overlooked the luxury villas and embassies of Garden City. Occasionally one could see an organ grinder with his monkey playing below. I had few toys, as was customary at the time, but I did have my soft toys and a small dolls' house. My blue bear was favourite, followed by Wilfred the rabbit, named after the character in a children's comic. The impression I give of rarely seeing my parents may be unfair, as I am relying solely on the memory of a three-or four-year-old. I do have a faint memory of my mother's presence in the nursery, a fleeting impression of fuss and anxiety in contrast to Nanny's stolid good humour. My father, being a journalist, worked long hours, but he may have been around more than I remember.

Some sketchy memories from this time . . .

. . . aged about three clinging to the bars of our wrought iron balcony watching a procession pass by, far below. The grown-ups towered above me and I suddenly realised that I, too, would one day be tall enough to lean on the balcony railings, instead of peering through them. Childhood would not last forever and one day I would be on equal terms with these powerful grown-ups. This is almost my first memory.

. . . on one journey from the gardens I encountered cruelty and madness for the first time. As we walked home a poor crazed Arab girl, unkempt, tearing at her hair and wailing, suddenly kicked me in the stomach. I was shocked and in pain for some time, but some of this was compensated for by the sight of Nanny in a rage accosting a policeman, and her subsequent loving care.

. . . on our way to the gardens we passed Kasr el Nil Barracks, (reputed to have been the most bug-ridden in the British Army and which stood where the Nile Hilton and Arab Union now stand). We would see soldiers, usually in their singlets, leaning out of the windows and waving to the passers-by. I remember flirting back, oblivious to the fact that all they could see was a small child in sun-bonnet and mosquito veil, being pushed in a buggy by a plump, plain nanny.

. . . one day, playing happily in the gardens, without warning we were assailed by a thick cloud of insects, hurling themselves and us children to the ground. It was like a hail of bullets. Nanny scooped me up and hurried home and later I learned it had been a plague of locusts.

. . . the large black pram that stood in the hall outside the nursery "in case God sends us another baby". But He never did and I was destined to be an only child. I believe my mother had a hysterectomy about this time.

Every summer my father took three months' leave and we travelled home to England, usually by Lloyd Triestino line to Italy and then overland via Venice and Paris by the Orient Express, until we acquired our smart, turquoise coupé Whippet, with a dickey at the back in which I sat. After that we drove across Europe. (Our previous car, as a matter of interest was unsuitable for long journeys as it was small and had three wheels. I would sit, cramped in the back seat, over the wheel.) Cars were still an uncommon sight in the quieter parts of Europe and our Whippet with its Egyptian number plate created a sensation. I have a few scrappy memories of these journeys: my doll Peter, who sat in the dickey with me; the poplar-lined roads of France; my mother's agitation when the car broke down and we had to stop at a dirty little hotel in France, which she was convinced was flea-ridden; the rain in Holland and my disappointment that the Dutch wore ordinary clothes and not the winged bonnets and clogs of my story books.

In England my parents had a flat, at first No. 2, Ruvigny Mansions on Putney Embankment. Cousin Beatie, twenty-three when I was born, newly married to her beloved David and living in Aberdeen, was summoned to London to look after me while my parents pursued their social and professional lives. Sometimes they rented a cottage on the East coast of Scotland and Beatie again joined us.

My fourth birthday was spent with Beatie and David in their flat in Aberdeen in Stanley Street. I remember going to buy a tricycle and I remember the sight of Granny Cheyne, Beatie's maternal grandmother, ensconced in her box bed in the living room and wielding great authority. (A box bed was a poor man's four-poster, with wooden box-like sides, wooden pillars and curtains behind which Granny could seek privacy.) Beatie had been considered to have married beneath her in marrying a working-class lad, but the most vivid memory I hold from this holiday was their evident love for one another – a love that was going to last into their old age.

Three months' annual leave must seem like undreamed-of luxury nowadays, and because of the long journey it was customary for men who worked in the Middle East to get home every two years. My father, self-employed, came home every year, leaving his sub-editor in charge and using his time in London to network his colleagues in Fleet Street.

All Change

When I was four we moved to Zamalek Buildings on Gezira. From the noisy, dirty centre of Cairo, we were now in the relative peace of the island, although we could hear the roar of the traffic on Sharia Fuad el Awal (Fuad the First, now Sharia 26 July) at the corner of our road.

The central part of Gezira was being developed at this time and apartment blocks were springing up. Zamalek Buildings, art deco, had only just been completed when we moved in, and the Italian architect, Signor Gavazi, and his voluptuous dark wife, lived on the first floor. She was the sister of my father's secretary, Lily, and I marvelled that they could be so different, for Lily was slim, fair, blue-eyed, a Botticelli Venus with that particular Arab huskiness in her voice, which is so attractive. She was, in fact, Syrian, and I adored her. If she visited the flat I would create a *fantasia* of decorations for the hall to welcome her.

The flat was light, airy and lifted the spirits. We were now near the Gezira Sporting Club, which was to be the centre of my social life for the next fifteen years, and Nanny took me daily to the playground there. Far from the noise of Midan Ismailia, we now walked through wide avenues, their pavements, as always in Cairo, covered in a film of fine sand blown in from the desert, in spite of the daily ministrations of the water carts. The roads were lined with scarlet flame of the forest trees and ethereal blue jacaranda. Bougainvillea spilled over garden walls and the giant ancient banyan tree, with its Arthur Rackham roots that stood near the entrance to the Club, always filled me with awe.

Now my mother played a larger part in my life, grooming and educating me. By the time I was four I could read and write, she taught me simple tunes on the piano and many evenings I would sing nursery rhymes, accompanied by her on the piano. As usual I joined my parents for a drink on the balcony before bedtime and I was now introduced to any grown-up guests. Sometimes they were distinguished visitors to Egypt and I remember meeting John Masefield, then the Poet Laureate. True journalist that he was, my father always impressed on me the privilege of any such meeting and in the future he was to take me to meet many celebrities. The one I remember most vividly at that time was Amy Johnson, pausing on one of her solo flights. She was the calm centre of a scurrying feverish clique of men and managed to give me a ravishing smile.

Dancing and riding lessons followed. For the former I went to the Ivy and Glen Moore Dance Academy (delicious Come Dancing name!). In fact it had a good reputation and I had lessons in classical ballet, but was chagrined that I couldn't do the splits.

Riding lessons were taken at the Mena House Hotel stables just below the Pyramids. Mena House was built as a hunting lodge for Napoleon III by the Khedive Ismail (meets were still being held there at the beginning of the twentieth century). The hotel was, and the old building still is, magnificent, opulent. The stables were across the road from the main entrance and Mr. Cullen, a wiry Australian, was my instructor. We would walk our horses across the road, past the brightly caparisoned camels and donkeys waiting to be hired, along the shady path by the tennis courts, with Mena's lush vegetable gardens and orchards to our right. Suddenly, we would be out in the dazzling sunshine, the wide-open spaces of the desert before us. Each time the sand dunes would have very slightly changed their shape as a result of the desert winds – unchanging was the black Bedouin tent, a hundred yards or so from the hotel grounds, probably a tourist attraction. We would bring our horses up to a trot and set off across the sand. They were exhilarating, wonderful rides and

Mr. Cullen, in spite of his brusque manner, was a kindly teacher.

Mena House played a big part in our lives and we often went out for the day and always for Christmas Day and Easter Day (egg hunts in the garden, presents of chocolate rabbits from the waiters). Mr. Gross, the Swiss manager, was a personal friend. He sent us a hamper of fresh vegetables and fruit from the gardens every Christmas. The old hotel is still much as it was in those days, except that until after the last war the main entrance was approached up wide steps to a terrace. The latter is now glassed in and is a restaurant. The old dining rooms were recently the same in all their splendour and there was still the smell of fresh baked bread in their entrance lobby. Modern buildings are now built on the old tennis courts to accommodate package tourists.

I felt completely at home in the large comfortable hotel and its exciting terraced grounds. I couldn't know that one of the unhappiest days of my life was soon to be spent there.

I began now to go to parties. Fancy dress ones were popular in the twenties and we would pore over pattern books choosing a suitable fancy dress. But parties could be an ordeal: crowded noisy affairs, where we were bullied by jolly grown-ups into playing endless games. The food was very special, but there was always the anxiety that one must behave well and remember to say 'thank you for having me' at the end of it all.

One special party was a children's party at the British Embassy. We sat at small tables round the edge of the ballroom. None of the usual party games. After tea the double doors were suddenly thrown open and in rode Father Christmas on a sleigh (led by what? I don't remember). He was accompanied by three fairies – real fairies I was assured, yet they were so large, the size of grown-ups. I couldn't make this out. The curtains on the stage were drawn back, revealing a treasure trove of presents. We each, in turn, went up and were given a present by a fairy. I chose a dolls' tea set and returned to my parents' table, suitably awed.

My socialisation was completed by joining the Brownies, but I didn't enjoy this much. The uniform was uncomfortable, the games (apart from Grandmothers' Footsteps) silly and my mother and I thought the injunctions sillier still. What was the point of learning to plait hair when most of us had the fashionable bob? Or learning how to make a milk pudding when we were not allowed into the kitchen at home? My mother would have none of such nonsense and I had to resort to lies about my prowess: 'Sorry, I left my pudding at home.'

Other memories from this time . . .

. . . Granny Seddall rocking me gently on her knee at bedtime and singing in her sweet high voice:

> 'Golden Slumbers kiss your eyes.
> Smiles awake you when you rise.
> Sleep pretty darling, do not cry
> And I will sing a lullaby.'

. . . having lunch one day in the dining room while my parents were out and Nanny putting on a record. Sayed, our cook, emerging from the kitchen and dancing merrily round the room, clicking his fingers above his head and grinning delightedly. This was *very* naughty and Nanny and I laughed immoderately.

. . . our large square gramophone with a horn, of which we were so very proud. Below the turntable were two doors opening on to a grille. I believed that a miniature fairy orchestra and singers were performing inside . . . the records we played: "Ain't She Sweet", "Lullaby of the Leaves", "Stormy Weather" . . .

. . . spending the day with cousins Peggy and Donald, which I often did, and the joys of eating suet puddings and writing our names on them with golden syrup. No such joys at home. There, a strict diet of brown bread, fruit and vegetables, white meat and daily yoghurt with stewed fruit. This diet is widely accepted now as ideal, but at the time it was adhered to only by faddists. And I have an idea it was confined to the nursery, as my father always enjoyed more robust fare.

. . . our *boab* (porter) who comported himself with dignity and courtesy, but whose red-rimmed eyes were so diseased that the flies clustered permanently around them.

. . . the beggars on the pavements, curled up asleep in their rags. The Arab women holding up their babies, whose limbs were mutilated – mutilated, it was said, by their parents so that they could be used for soliciting alms.

. . . the better-off working-class Arab women in their long black robes, their *yashmaks* attached to their head-dresses by elaborate brass nose-pieces. The *yashmaks* glittering with brass coins denoting the amount of their dowries. Their kohl-rimmed eyes, the henna'd palms of their hands, hands sometimes tattooed, the glimpses of bright colours from under the black robes.

. . . the death of Ali, our *suffragi* (house boy) who died swiftly of septicaemia from a cut on a sardine tin. This sudden death from so simple a cause horrified me. It was my first experience of death and it was followed by two more. My beloved Foxtrot, the safe elderly horse I rode at Mena, had to be put down, but my mother assured me that he and Ali had gone to heaven. Then Granny Taylor, my paternal grandmother died in Scotland. Her death didn't affect me personally, as I hardly remembered her, but I was touched by my father's quiet grief.

. . . being fitted for new clothes by the Greek dressmaker who periodically visited us for this purpose. She would come for one or two days. The material would have been bought at Chemla or Cicurel, the two large department stores, and the designs chosen from a pattern book. I would stand patiently while she, her mouth bristling with pins, turned me around, tucking here, tucking there. I loved clothes enough to endure all this without complaint.

Clothes were important in our family. My father, short for a man, always had his suits made in Saville Row. My mother, also petite, bought her dresses each summer at a Mayfair dress agency, where she could find models going for a song. As for me, in addition to the dresses made by our Greek seamstress, Aunt Vi, my godmother, sent out delicious confections of party dresses that she had made. I particularly remember a deep pink georgette dress trimmed with rosebuds round neck, waist and hem, and a white and yellow organdie dress with deep frills at the hem. To go to parties I would wear with them white socks and black dance pumps, my ankles criss-crossed with black elastic. (Aunt Vi's husband, Frank, had by this time died of tuberculosis. She was a fine needlewoman and had opened a small dress shop in Dublin, which was proving a success.)

For our summer leave we would, as usual, travel to England across Europe and stay in London, this time in a mansion flat in Buckingham Gate, which we rented. Sometimes there would be a visit to Aberdeen.

One summer my mother and I spent time at the Harmsworths' home in Hyde Park Gardens. Lady Harmsworth was, I think, sister-in-law to Lord Rothermere, the then proprietor of *The Daily Mail* and my father's boss. She was Irish like my mother and the two women became close friends. When we arrived they would scamper up the staircase, giggling and chattering to continue their gossip upstairs. I would be left to wander round the impressive house, from the busy kitchens in the basements full of friendly staff, parrots in cages hanging from the ceiling, to the first floor ballroom where I once surprised some young Harmsworths and friends dancing to a wind-up gramophone. The dining room on the ground floor overlooked the garden at the back and the refectory table was always fully laid, so that anyone could drop in for lunch. Sometimes we were three or four, sometimes a dozen or more. There I learned to join in adult conversation, there I learned to peel an artichoke correctly. And in the garden at the back I learned to ride a bike on their son's bicycle. Off the dining room was an ante-room where the family relaxed with friends. In this room Lady Harmsworth gave me first editions of the Louisa M. Alcott books, which I treasured and loved, but which invariably got lost in my many travels.

Lady Harmsworth was one day to play an unwitting part in the final break-up of my parents' marriage.

One summer my father went home to England on his own, leaving my mother and me in Cairo. Even to my five-year-old mind it seemed a strange decision to make. It may have been a question of expense as it was the year of the Wall Street crash and everyone was affected by it. Or my mother may have had a sinister motive in persuading him to go without us.

There was a new and frequent visitor to the flat this summer; a Parsee journalist colleague of my father's who was in Egypt on an assignment. He was lean, dark and good-looking, with a Ronald Colman moustache. To my disgust, my mother fluttered around him, laughing in her bird-like way at his every joke. I distrusted him. And this was unusual for me, as until then I had on the whole an innocent trust of all adults, who seemed both benevolent and admiring. "Radish" (I couldn't pronounce his name of Ardishir) did his best to win me over with funny letters, conjuring tricks and presents, but I remained stubbornly unimpressed.

One day the world was over-turned. While playing in the nursery I overheard my mother and Nanny having a quarrel. This had never happened before. I only heard clearly my mother's words: 'None of your business.'

Within days Nanny had left. I was told she was taking her annual holiday in Syria, which this year had so far been denied her.

I only remember feeling bewildered and lost, uncomprehending, but part of me must have been extremely angry for soon I became unmanageable, demanding and naughty.

My mother moved in to sleep in the nursery with me and began to indulge me. I could choose what clothes to wear, for instance, but this idea was abandoned when it became clear I only wanted to wear Aunt Vi's party dresses.

As an interim measure it was decided that I should share the English nanny to Pamela and Sally Jarman, who lived upstairs. Pamela was my age and a close friend, Sally her younger sister. Each day we all went to the Club and in the evenings I would be delivered home in time for the balcony drinks. Sometimes I spent the night with the Jarmans and this was always fun.

But this arrangement nearly ended in disaster.

We went daily to the swimming pool. In the children's dressing room there was a large basket filled with dried gourds which served as water-wings. One day I got the last pair of gourds in the basket. They were cracked. The nanny noticed this, but decided that I would be safe in them provided I stayed by the edge of the pool, holding on to the side rail. She gave me strict instructions to do so, without explaining her reasons, and for a while I was prepared to obey her. But I soon got fed up with watching my friends playing ring-a-ring-a-roses in the middle of the pool and struck out to join them.

By this time, of course, the gourds had filled with water and I began to sink. It was a not unpleasant sensation, lying peacefully on my back, the water gently rippling above me. Through the ripples I could see the Jarman nanny frantically calling for help. Then all went black and the next thing I remember was being on the edge of the pool with my woman rescuer leaning over me. I was stunned by the incident but didn't burst into tears until I saw my mother on the drawing room balcony anxiously asking what was the matter with me.

That was the end of the Jarman nanny arrangement. My mother's theories about the obtuseness of the average English nanny were confirmed and she decided to try an Armenian nanny.

Following the Turkish massacres of the Armenians in 1918, a large number of children found their way to Egypt and took refuge in an orphanage in Old Cairo. Some were now of an age to earn their livings and there was a glut of Armenian nannies on the market.

Alice was my first Armenian nanny, but she didn't stay, and two more came and went in fast succession. I had continued to be rebellious, rude, angry, uncontrollable – and young as the Armenian girls were, traumatised and institutionalised as they were, they were unable to cope with me. The fourth nanny, Lucy, stayed. She was a plump, good-humoured girl and I took to her.

One day Lucy took me to the orphanage to visit a friend of hers who suffered from "sleeping sickness". It was a sober occasion and the building was stark and Dickensian. The dormitories were bare except for rows of iron bedsteads. I was taken aback by these spartan conditions and it is chastening to report that I was reminded of them when, as a social worker in the Fifties, I was to visit one of the old workhouses still in use for the elderly and homeless. Except that at the Elephant and Castle there were four, not two, rows of beds to a dormitory and the residents were supervised by women in navy uniform with bunches of keys at their waists. Men and women were strictly segregated.

My mother woke me one morning to announce it was a special day and we were all going to the club. It was Umpire Day, she said. Umpire Day? I knew about umpires. They sat on very high chairs watching tennis players on the courts. So I supposed we were going to watch the tennis, but what was so special about that?

When we arrived at the club we made for the race course which was crowded with people, including servicemen in uniform, Indian Sikhs in turbans, Egyptians and Sudanese, Scouts, Guides, Brownies and Cubs, all in uniform. Of course a military band played. It was *Empire* Day and we were to watch all kinds of shows and exhibitions and races.

This was my first introduction to the concept of the British Empire and like most children of my generation I was to become proud of our achievements in holding dominion over so much of the world's surface. It was clearly *self-evident* that we were very special indeed. In my youth it was a simple article of faith that we, the English, were *ipso facto* better than any other race. ("English" we children called ourselves in Egypt – British-ness seemed too large a concept and we thought of the Scots, Welsh and Irish as coming under the umbrella of the "English".) We were to become proud of our fighting forces, of our democratic and judicial systems. We seemed to triumph at all we undertook, whether it be at sport or in business or at war. I would only add that, although it is fashionable these days to decry the British Empire, the British civil servants whom I was to meet and know seemed to be hard-working men of integrity, who loved Egypt and served the country well.

This sounds as if we strutted about arrogantly. In fact we rarely thought or spoke of the subject. We simply had this inner certainty about ourselves. We admired some of the qualities of other nationalities, but pitied them that they couldn't belong to our superior tribe.

As Flanders and Swann were to sing many years later in their satirical *Song of Patriotic Prejudice:* "The English, the English, The English are Best . . ."

The Club needs to be described for it was the centre of our lives as children and adolescents and it was indeed remarkable. There were other sporting clubs in Cairo: at Heliopolis and Ma'adi, both Cairo suburbs, and on Gezira there was also the Willcocks, smaller and with fewer amenities than the Gezira Sporting Club.

At Gezira every imaginable sport was catered for, from bowls and croquet to polo and racing. There were about a dozen tennis courts, squash courts, a golf course, polo fields, a cricket pitch, and a swimming pool.

The clubhouse was at the centre of the club and had comfortable rooms in which to relax and rooms for bridge and other card games. Every Saturday night there would be a dinner-dance. The jazz band would be made up of servicemen.

The clubhouse led on to the tea gardens, the hub of social life. All day the small tables would be occupied by members chatting and clapping their hands for tea or drinks. The gardens overlooked the cricket pitch and, as most of the British men worked long mornings but not in the afternoons, the sound of bat on ball would be accompanied by the chink of teacups. After dark, the coloured fairy lights that laced the trees would be lit.

The tea gardens also led to the children's playground. In keeping with the high standards of the rest of the club, we had every sort of amusement laid on: sand pits, swings, seesaws and a wonderful maypole-style contraption whereby one could swing oneself high up in the air. There was also a building which housed every sort of acrobatic need. The nannies grouped themselves in chairs according to nationality and gossiped. We were allowed the run of the playground with minimal supervision that I remember. (On one occasion, sitting near the Armenian group, I overheard one nanny boast that she had been "home" to England with "her family". She told her wondering friends that in England the English serve in the shops and even have work as cleaners. She was not believed!)

On Fridays the nannies took their charges to the racecourse where there was the weekly race meeting. The attraction was the military band which played on the opposite side of the racecourse to the grandstand. The nannies positioned themselves as closely as possible to the musicians so that they could flirt with them. We amused ourselves as best we could, occasionally rushing over to the railings to watch the horses thundering past.

But most of our time was spent in the playground, until the warmer weather came and we moved to the swimming pool. After my near-drowning, Uncle Don taught me to swim and it wasn't long before I could swim and dive fearlessly.

In later years the games we played in the pool were to become adventurous. We would throw a piastre in the water and dive for it. Another game was Follow My Leader. We were all expert swimmers and divers and all copied the leader in the swallow dive, jack-knife, straight dive, honeypot jump. We also had a version of water polo, which consisted of getting the ball by fair means or foul. My unique trick was to jump from the top board, dropping with deadly accuracy on to the ball and snatching it from someone.

It has been claimed that the Club was for the British exclusively. This is simply not true. The British formed the majority of members, but a great many other nationalities were represented. Needless to say, the applicant was usually a successful member of his profession or business and had to be "put up".

The only racism I encountered at this time was, interestingly enough, against the French. There was a large contingent of French children in the playground, who kept to themselves. Cousin Peggy organised an "army" to fight the French and I remember, skirt tucked into my knickers and wielding a homemade wooden sword, whooping war cries from the safety of a bush. The French wisely ignored us and we soon became distracted by other pleasures.

We envied the French, as a matter of fact. For their mid-morning break they were given crusty French bread and chunks of plain chocolate. We had nothing and had to wait hungrily for lunch. Maybe that lay behind our animosity, or was it some ancient tribal enmity?

The summer came to an end. My father returned from his leave and it was decided that we should move again.

This time we moved to Gezira House, within a quick walking distance of the Club. It was an old building, large, rambling, three-sided round a courtyard in which the *boabs* sat. They were particularly devout and seemed religiously to answer the muezzin's five-daily calls to prayer, kneeling on their prayer mats, bending foreheads to floor.

Our flat was larger than the last, high ceilinged. The rooms all led off a big round central hall, which we used as dining room. My nursery overlooked the Gezira Casino, a long, single-storied building in the Moorish style with gardens and fountains at the rear. (It has now gone and been replaced by the hideous modern Anglican Cathedral. The latter, in turn, has replaced the beautiful cathedral designed by Gilbert Scott on the banks of the Nile, which was demolished to make way for a new bridge and the TV Centre.)

From the master bedroom could be seen another modern apartment block in which my friend Joan was to live. Behind that the "Lotfallah Palace", now the Marriott Hotel. The palace was another extravagance built by the Khedive Ismail for the Empress Eugenie when she and Napoleon visited Egypt. When we were there it was occupied by the Syrian Prince Lotfallah and his family. We had, in fact, been inside the palace. The small princes went to the Ivy and Glen Moore dancing school and the annual dancing display had been held there.

Pamela Jarman and I didn't dance on that occasion, but stood at each side of the stage, dressed as marquis (me) and marquise. We met and bowed and curtseyed between each item. I was immensely excited by my costume: a sprigged satin jacket with frills at neck and wrists, pink satin knickerbockers, white socks, black buckled shoes. And a powdered wig! My face was heavily made up, completed by a beauty spot. After the display, we threaded our way, in pairs, through the tea tables occupied by our admiring parents. I walked with one of the princes, who confessed to liking me and suggested we might marry one day. My first proposal!

Soon after our arrival at Gezira House my mother organised my first party, a large affair to which all my friends were invited. My father was said to have brought back a suitcase of toys from Woolworth's for there were presents for everyone, including a fairy doll for me, which graced the top of the Christmas tree. But I didn't enjoy a minute of that party. My mother fluttered around organising games, my father (unusually) was at home, gloomily standing on the fringes. We were an unhappy family, although I couldn't understand exactly why.

I woke up in the middle of the night on Christmas Eve, with my mother in my parents' double bed. At the foot of the bed were two pillowcases bulging with presents. Presumably my father had taken to sleeping in his dressing room. When I woke he was leaning over us (I now suspect that he was drunk), accusing my mother, among other things, of telling "Radish" some confidential information about his work. My mother slipped out of bed to telephone Uncle Don for help and my father asked me how I would like to 'have Radish as a Daddy.' Terrifying! Soon Uncle Don appeared and dragged my father from the bedroom.

Next morning we should, as usual, have gone to Mena House as a family for the day. Instead, my mother and I went there with "Radish". I have a vivid memory of the two adults going down the stairs, my mother chattering as usual, myself drearily trailing behind. My father stood at the front door, watching us, and I felt helplessly bewildered that my all-powerful father could not stop all this happening.

I have no memory of that Christmas Day at Mena.

Soon after Christmas, my father moved to the National Hotel, 'to be near his office'. In March my mother and I left for England by sea.

Unheard-of for the sophisticated Taylors to travel by P&O with other bourgeois English families, rather than to go overland through Europe. And to go in March, through the treacherous Bay of Biscay, when my mother was such a poor sailor! This finally confirmed for me that the world was now upside-down.

We had a cat, a feral stray we had acquired, who was devoted to my mother but who disliked me as much as I disliked him. On our last day in Cairo I found myself hugging

Pussy in a paroxysm of grief at leaving him behind. But even at that young age I puzzled at my behaviour and half understood it wasn't the loss of the cat I was grieving, but something larger and unnameable.

We arrived in England to a snowstorm, which enchanted me, and went straight to Dorset to join Aunt Rosie and the cousins.

Aunt Rosie was my mother's elder sister and married to Donald Llewellyn, who worked for the Shell Company of Egypt. She had come home with my cousins, Peggy and Donald, to put them to school, leaving Uncle Don in Cairo. She had rented a small pebbledash house in Parkstone, a suburb of Poole. It was an ugly house, wedged between a row of small shops on one side and large, detached houses with laurel-fringed drives on the other. But it was opposite the gates to Poole Park and near Uncle Don's many relatives. The Llewellyns were an old Dorset family and there was a large clan of them. It was always good to be with my cousins and I was soon enjoying life again.

My mother began to make frequent trips to London 'to see Lady Harmsworth'. In fact she was meeting "Radish" and my aunt was later to reproach herself that she hadn't seen through this ruse.

One day my mother went to London and did not return. At all.

I understand I had a tempestuous screaming fit: 'Where's she gone? Where's she gone?' I began to have daytime fears and nightmares and Aunt Rosie moved me in to sleep with Peggy and Donald. As an added comfort she would light the nursery fire at bedtime and we would fall asleep to the flickering flames.

Once the emotional storm was over, I calmed down as though I had learned that temper tantrums and bad behaviour didn't pay, and I lived for the day. I tended to retreat into books and into a personal dream world and was for many years to be wary and circumspect with adults. I assumed the mantle of the good little girl with them. With my peers I felt free and confident and, thanks to their friendship and companionship and their sheer high spirits, I look back on my childhood as comparatively happy.

I was also blessed in the mother-substitutes who were to care for me in the future, all of whom between them gave me affection and encouragement and restored my self-esteem.

And Peggy (nine) and Donald (seven) were perfect companions. Peggy, imaginative and a born leader, thought up fascinating games and Donald and I followed amiably in her wake. Aunt Rosie must have been unusually tolerant for we often took over the house. On one occasion we turned the sitting room into a shop. Furniture was moved appropriately, hours were spent cutting out advertisements to use as stock, further hours were spent making our own currency with paper, pencil and scissors. Then days were spent trading.

The dining room was frequently occupied for a game called Surprises. Two of us would plan a surprise for the third. It might be a puppet show (Peggy had made a puppet theatre) or a trip round the floor on a doormat, stopping now and again for a treat. The worst surprise was "tortures" when one was pinned down on the window seat and tickled.

Peggy formed a secret society with several neighbourhood children and we swore eternal loyalty and secrecy on an old goldfish bowl. The main purpose of this society seemed to be to stalk the Grammar School boys through the park, which we did from the safety of the shrubberies. Echoes of our anti-French "war".

I was now nearly seven years old and had never been to school, so it was decided that I should join my cousins at St. Hilary's, a small prep school in Parkstone run by a Colonel and Mrs. Martyn. I proudly set off every morning in my royal blue and gold uniform, with my cousins, on the bus. The only lessons I remember are geography, when I struggled to make sense of the map of Great Britain, and the first lesson of each day when we spent half-an-hour learning to spell a new list of words. Otherwise I remember racing round the many bushes and flowerbeds in the garden during break.

I was taught a salutary lesson in compassion. One of the boys in our form, Horace, was "simple". His mother invited several friends to his birthday party. When we arrived, we were the only guests who had turned up. Horace's mother was touchingly relieved and grateful; and Aunt Rosie, when we returned home, highly indignant when she heard what had happened and of the hurt that must have been inflicted on child and mother.

On my seventh birthday in June, while we were having lunch, I suddenly saw my father walking past the dining room window. He had turned up unexpectedly as a surprise, to my intense delight, and soon after took me to stay with my mother's eldest sister, Aunt Vi, in Ireland.

I was not to see or hear from my mother for the next four years. She was rarely, if ever, mentioned in my presence. The subject was taboo. The scandal was, of course, well known in Cairo. My friends were told by their parents that my mother had died and was not to be referred to, although I was unaware of this at the time. Conspiracy of silence.

As for me, the new submissive me, I formed a protective carapace, was to feel few intense emotions for some years and stoically accepted whatever the grown-ups planned for me. This is not to say that, paradoxically, I didn't get a great deal of pleasure from life.

My Parents

So far my parents have been described from the viewpoint of a small child with the aid of a fragmented, selective memory. It seems fair now to take a more objective view of them.

Daisy was in her late thirties at the time of the separation. She was petite, elegant in the fashion of the Twenties, pretty, intelligent with a quick Irish wit. She spoke French fluently ('You are not civilised, darling, unless you speak and write French') and she was musical. She was a Fabian Socialist and feminist and also an unutterable snob ('Every sort of snob, darling'). I believe this snobbery sprang, as it usually does, from low self-esteem, but it was also part of her search for excellence and refinement in all things. She may have been considered pretentious, for in an effort to disguise her Irish brogue she had developed a strangulated ugly "posh" accent. Although she showed compassion towards those less fortunate than herself, she couldn't disguise her contempt for the bourgeois English families who sought to create another Aldershot or Surbiton in places like Ma'adi. She rarely went to the Club, but she regularly rode at Mena. Mostly her days were spent either working with my father or in the salons of Cairo. Her closest friends were Lucienne Fischer, a sharp-witted elegant Parisienne, Lydia Golding, who with her solicitor husband had fled the revolution in Russia, and Edith Smyth, married to an American. In spite of her gifts and advantages, Daisy must have been deeply flawed, for she ended her life as a long-standing alcoholic, living in poverty. The seeds were there in my early childhood. I remember the "nerves" she was prone to.

Daisy was the youngest of three sisters whose father was a Protestant Anglo-Irishman, the son of a clergyman. He himself was an officer in the Royal Irish Constabulary and was to become a Chief Constable. Daisy's mother was an Irish Roman Catholic, a Geoghegan, a member of one of the "six Tribes" to come over to Galway from Northern France in the thirteenth century, and who dominated the town for the next two hundred years. Daisy's parents separated and the girls were sent to board at a convent in Southampton, only going home for a holiday once a year. Daisy did well at school and stayed on to teach French and music for a while. Then she took a secretarial course at "Mrs. Hoster's" in Kensington and got a job as secretary to my father when he was editor of *Great Britain and the Near East.*

My father told me that when she sat down to take dictation from him, her feet didn't touch the floor, and he fell deeply in love with this petite, pretty girl.

In 1917, in the middle of the Great War, my parents were married by special licence at Brompton Oratory (they were both Roman Catholics, at least nominally). The next day my father was posted to Palestine and they were not to meet again for five years, when Daisy joined her husband in Cairo. A year later I was born.

Who knows why they married in such a hurry. What did her family in Ireland make of the telegram she sent to them: 'Married Mr. Taylor yesterday. Coming home'? She had a deep affection for my father, admired and respected him, but one has these days to wonder about the sexual side of the marriage. She was sexually inexperienced when she married, may even have been ignorant of the "facts of life" in spite of having two married sisters. Such matters were not discussed. When she met her *'coup de foudre'* (her words), in the person of Ardisheer, she was unable to resist him.

Philip was in his early fifties at the time of the separation. By then he had managed a music hall in Aberdeen and been an actor and a teacher, but had then turned to journalism. To read of his professional achievements before, during and after the 1914-18 War is bewildering. He had initiated and been managing editor of several publications, both in Fleet Street and the Middle East, as well as acting as local correspondent for newspapers and agencies. He had been awarded the Order of the Nile for services to Anglo-Egyptian relations and was now a hard-working respected journalist.

As a young man he had fallen in love before. I was to meet the daughter of an ex-girlfriend and he also fell for Molly Preston, half-sister of Robert Graves, then teaching in Egypt. When in middle age he confessed to her his youthful ardour, she said "Oh Philip, had I but known!' I have always suspected that one reason he had not married earlier was because he had to support his crippled brother's daughters, Beatie and Lena. He adored my mother and once told me she was the only woman he had ever loved.

His appearance, as I remember him, was of a short man, smartly dressed. He was going bald, sported an eyeglass and had fierce eyebrows to rival those of Dennis Healey. Under the eyebrows were shrewd, humorous eyes.

In middle age Philip was serious, deep thinking and moralistic, but had an impish sense of humour which never left him. I have often seen him laughing so hard at someone's story that he would double up, losing his eyeglass in the process. He would deftly catch it and screw it back in once the convulsion was over. He was well loved and would never turn anyone away who was in trouble. Indeed he once travelled to Upper Egypt where he had heard there was an English woman who had run out of money and was living on the charity of the Egyptians. He brought her back to Cairo, employed her as a secretary, and she was to become a close family friend.

Philip now took his parenting role seriously. I had always known he loved me and now we were to become close friends. If he had a fault, as far as I was concerned, it was that he was totally incapable of discussing emotional issues. Only once were the barriers to come down when we had a flaming row in my teenage years.

Christina Taylor, my grandmother.

Officer Cadet Philip Taylor, Artists Rifles. 1916.

With my mother. 1924.

Members of the press outside Tutankhamun's tomb.
November 1922. *Far left: my mother. Second from right:
Arthur Merton (The Times), then my father, then Philip
O'Farrell.*

Cousin Donald Llewellyn. 1929.

With cousin Jane. Gezira House. 1932.

Ireland

So, in a new relationship, my father and I travelled to Ireland so that I could spend the summer holidays with Aunt Vi, my mother's eldest sister. We were to become dependant on the kindness and generosity of many women who cared for me, and one advantage for me was that I became remarkably adaptable to new circumstances.

Aunt Vi was living outside Cork with her second husband, another barrister, a merry red-haired man, and her three sons, Eddy, John and Frank. The boys were in their teens and seemed like grown-ups to me, and we led our separate lives.

They lived in a double-fronted, wisteria-covered Georgian house with a large garden, which sloped steeply down to the estuary. From the front door we could see the ferries sailing to and from England. At the back of the house was a walled kitchen garden with a gnarled apple tree in the middle.

The house was furnished with the barest necessities (cousin John slept on a mattress on the floor, his bedside light connected to the ceiling light. And mattresses on the floor were *not* trendy in the Thirties). Aunt Vi had no domestic help: she and Granny Seddall were up before breakfast, laying the fires and starting on the housework.

In spite of these stringencies at home, the boys went to public school and Uncle Jack had a yacht moored at Crosshaven. Every weekend we went sailing, Uncle Jack in white flannels, navy jacket and yacht cap, the boys crewing for him. I had always loved being on board large liners, but was afraid of boarding this small boat the first time. Aunt Vi took me below and taught me to play Patience. By the time the game was over we were under way, and as soon as I went on deck I was infected with the pleasure of sailing.

I befriended Eamonn, the boy who lived with his widowed mother on the other side of the lane. He had a friend, John, and the three of us played together most days. The boys, in appearance, could have walked out of the pages of *Just William* and we were in fact quite naughty. They taught me to smoke, among other things. Eamonn would steal his mother's cigarettes, light one by the votive candle which stood in her bedroom before a statue of the Sacred Heart and we would then hide in the bushes of the terraced garden and chain smoke. One of Eamonn's ideas was to steal and hide his mother's silver in the garden – not for any other reason than that it would be a dare. We were, of course, found out and severely reprimanded.

Mostly, we played among the shrubberies in the terraced garden or up the apple tree. The latter became in turn a house, ship, train or bus. I used to jump out of the apple tree time and again in the hope that suddenly I would fly.

We went swimming at the public baths in Cork and I was much taken with one of the bus conductors. He would come up to us and whisper, 'I scream, you scream, we all scream for ice-cream!' I thought this the height of wit.

Soon the end of the holidays came and my father and I travelled back to Cairo.

A New Family . . .

When we returned to Cairo it was to find that Aunt Rosie and Uncle Don were to share the Gezira House flat with us. Peggy and Donald had been left in England to board at St. Hilary's.

I was immediately sent to board at the English School, which pleased me greatly as my friends and heroines, Elsie and Vivian Vernon Jarvis, were daygirls there. I was soon to regret my enthusiasm.

The English School had been founded for the education of those English children whose parents either couldn't afford to send them to school in England or didn't wish to do so. In fact, despite its name, English children were in the minority at the time. As usual in Egypt, almost every nationality was represented.

The main day-school at that time was in Bulaq, a poor quarter of Cairo just across the Bulaq Bridge from Gezira, in which there must have been a substantial British community for both the Methodist and Presbyterian churches were also situated there.

The school was forbidding with its asphalt playground and stark buildings. The lessons were academically demanding, the discipline strict. The worst memory I have of the school was the punishment meted out to the boy who was always bottom of the class (we were graded, at the age of seven, weekly). It was clear to us children that he was simple, incapable of thinking quickly. Once, when he repeatedly couldn't find a town on the map on the wall, the geography teacher cleared the desks. The girls were made to stand at the sides, the boys at the back of the room. They were given tennis balls to throw at the hapless victim, who had been made to stand on Miss G's desk. Shocked and miserable as we were, none of us mentioned this incident to our parents.

The boarding houses were situated out at Helwan, considered to be a health resort because it was on the edge of the desert and boasted sulphur baths. The buildings were large, spacious and gracious and there were at least flowerbeds in the grounds. The boys and girls had separate playgrounds and were separated in the house: boys upstairs, girls on the ground floor.

There were two large girls' dormitories. I was one of the youngest there, together with Bertha and Nellie, also seven. The older girls wouldn't let us out of bed in the mornings until they were fully dressed, so we three had a mad scramble to get ready in time. Then into the playground to skip before breakfast. After breakfast we were bussed to the station for the train to Cairo. We behaved disgracefully on the train, hanging out of the windows and invading each others' territories. I don't know how we did not have an accident.

Lessons were manageable and I was usually near the top of the class (we moved desks according to test results each week), but there were some miseries to be dealt with in Helwan, including a heavy homework load.

There was one particular supper on the menu which unfailingly made me sick, but I was always made to eat it. I can still remember the smell of the soup rising from the kitchen. I began to wet my bed. I argued that if I could go to the lavatory in the night this wouldn't happen, but this wasn't allowed as it might wake Matron who slept next door. As a punishment my eye-catching bright yellow pyjamas were hung over the balcony overlooking the boys' playground 'so that the boys can know how naughty you have been'.

As ever in childhood, we did have fun too. On Guy Fawkes Night we built a huge bonfire in the desert, with fireworks, and we sang 'Show me the way to go home' through the streets of Helwan afterwards. We had a riotous Christmas party. Often we went for wonderful long walks along the rocky escarpments of the desert. Nellie, Bertha and I played innocent games such as "fairy tea parties" using the leaves and honey of nasturtiums. During the sugar cane season we would buy some at the school gates, strip the bark and chew the sticks until the sweet, sticky juice ran down our chins.

But I was, deep down, very unhappy at the English School and when I eventually told my father this, to my astonishment he said I need not go back, but could instead go to "Madame Morin's", a French school run by Madame and her husband René. The school, whose proper name was the Zamalek School, had two classes for English children and was situated on the north side of Gezira on the banks of the Nile, within walking distance of the flat. Several of my friends were already there and, with a great sense of relief, I joined them.

Life was transformed again. I was back at home, living in a family, however unusually composed. It can't have been easy for the Llewellyns to share a home with us. My father was in a deep depression and seeking distraction in his work. He was nearly twenty years older than Uncle Don and his ideas on bringing up a child were Edwardian, whereas the Llewellyns were liberal, avant garde parents, who encouraged debate and free thought in their young. I was to benefit from this in the future, but at this stage Aunt Rosie and Uncle Don kept their counsel and my memory is of subdued meals and a distance kept between the two halves of the household.

For some reason a governess was engaged for me, although I was at school. She did teach me the piano, but the poor woman's banalities at the lunch table so irritated my father that she had to go. (I was beginning to learn the subtle niceties of class distinction. Governesses ate with us; nannies ate in the nursery and the servants ate on the roof or in the cafés, unless they were lucky enough to have their families living with them and not in their villages.)

Aunt Rosie began to take over the role of my mother. She had told my father that she would look after me but could not be expected to love me. I can't have been a lovable child at this time and she must have been extremely angry with my mother for dumping me. However, she was always very relaxed, gentle and understanding, and I believe that her affection eventually deepened into something akin to love.

Aunt Rosie was the second of the three Seddall sisters. She was a small woman like my mother and had a congenitally displaced hip which caused her to limp badly, in spite of a built-up surgical shoe. It was such a familiar sight to see her walking along slowly, listing over to the left with every step, that it never occurred to me that this was a handicap or might be painful. It amazed me when a friend told me that she and her mother felt sorry for her. She always looked content with her lot, never happier than when all the family were around her, when her large blue eyes would shine with pleasure. She was philosophical, Aunt Rosie, and an amused smile rarely left her lips.

Uncle Don had met her when he was stationed in Athlone during the Troubles, an officer in the Royal Engineers, and had married her by the end of the Great War. He had been a schoolteacher before the war, did not, or could not, return to that (there was mass unemployment after the war) and so took his wife and small baby, Peggy, out to Alexandria. Aunt Vi and her family were already there in the hope that the Egyptian climate would be good for Uncle Frank's tuberculosis. My parents were in Cairo, so all three sisters found themselves in Egypt.

But work was hard to find in Egypt also and my father recommended Uncle Don for a job as a clerk with the Shell Company. With his high intelligence and experience in the

Royal Engineers, he soon rose to executive status and by the time we were living together he was head of the bitumen department of the company. Within the next few years he was to invent a new form of road surface. He built two aerodromes in the Sudan and – much more importantly – the famous Desert Road, starting out from Mena House and into the Sahara. It had been thought that it was impossible to build an asphalt road across shifting sand and this was the first time it had been done. The road proved to be a vital supply route during the desert battles in the Second World War and it has been argued that if we had lost those, we would have lost the whole war to the Germans. It was a narrow road, just room for two vehicles to pass, and may have been cursed by many servicemen in the war, but it was a feat of engineering in its time and probably saved lives.

In looks Uncle Don was a tall man, over six foot, loose-limbed and athletic. He had a sensual mouth and moustache, a large hooked nose ('we must have Jewish blood somewhere,' he would say) and a thatch of black hair, which he tried to control with Brylcreem. He was very left-wing in his politics and outspoken in his views. He was a philanderer, a fact that was apparently tolerated, with amused long-suffering, by his wife. I think he may not have been popular with the majority of the British community in Cairo, because they were, for the most part, conservative and conventional and disapproved of his liberal views and behaviour.

But as far as I was concerned he was the perfect uncle. He was great fun, entered into our interests, was to devise exciting excursions and holidays for us, had a great sense of humour and a fund of good stories and songs. (I secretly wished that my older, more serious father could be more like him. It was only in later years that I discovered that my father also had a light-hearted, amusing side).

Uncle Don had a deep bass voice and would burst into song with the least encouragement. Some of the best memories of those days were of lying in bed in my nursery going to sleep to the sound of singing round the piano in the drawing room. At that time young men in large British companies were not allowed to marry before a certain age, or before they had attained a certain status (cousin Lena and Ian married secretly in their twenties), and most evenings Uncle Don and Aunt Rosie had open house for the "Shell boys". Up to half a dozen usually came: Edward Mayne, a beautiful young man who was later to become Managing Director of Shell UK, his sister Isa, George Duthoit, who accompanied the singing, Ruth Eppler, a woman doctor, and "Davey" Jones are the ones I remember. Often I joined them before bedtime. The songs were mainly from the Students' Song Book: negro spirituals, sea shanties, folk songs: *Oh Shenandoah, Oh My Darling Clementine, Riding Down to Rio,* etc. Good rousing songs one could sing with gusto.

I fell in love with Davey Jones. In his early twenties, he was outrageously good-looking in a dark, Celtic way. He seemed to like me too and would come and sit on my bed and chat. In our more cynical modern times we would question his interest in an eight-year-old girl, but I believe it was innocent (children can usually tell) and was certainly regarded as such. It soon became an understood subject for banter that we would marry when I was old enough. My night prayers were now reduced to 'Please God, let me marry Davey Jones or . . .' (as realism crept in) 'someone like him.'

I acquired some tortoises. A wrinkled old man used to stand at the club gates, with a dirty satchel slung round his neck, selling goods. It might be cheap jewellery or greeting cards or toys. He hit on the idea of tortoises and his satchel would swarm with the poor creatures struggling to get out. Just about all my friends at the club bought some. I brought home three which we christened Seamus (my aunt's choice of name), Mary and "the baby", because he was so tiny. "The baby" soon died but the other two sometimes came in from the balcony, where they were kept, to join the evening parties. Seamus was the sociable one and wandered around curiously. Mary sat miserably near the window and we thought she was shy, but the poor thing was literally out of her element. We had suspected something was unusual when she insisted always on sitting in the bowl of water I put out for them. The truth was discovered when I took the tortoises to the club for "exercise" on the edge of the flooded cricket pitch. Mary swam happily into the middle of the water and had to be fetched back to go home. We realised that she was, after all, a turtle. After that I took her for a swim as often as possible. As rain is almost unknown in Egypt, the sports fields had regularly to be flooded, so there were opportunities for her to have a good time.

My father was never at the evening parties. He was home every day for two o'clock lunch, followed by a short siesta before returning to his office, but he spent his evenings out. He might be working, or propping up the bar at the Turf Club, and would later eat out, either at the club or at Tommy's Bar opposite or with friends.

The Turf Club was founded in 1893 as a gentlemen's club (for the British of course) and my father was to be seen in the bar every lunchtime and evening of his Cairo life. It was there that he met his friends and colleagues and used to say that it was there that he picked up all the important political and social news. His "bits of paper" were well known. If he heard some snippet that was newsworthy, he would fish into a pocket, bring out a bit of paper and scribble away.

(There was to be one noteworthy and providential occasion in the Fifties when he did not go to the club at lunchtime. He had been due to meet *The Times* correspondent there for a drink, but the latter rang him up to say he had heard there would be trouble in the town and suggested my father went to his flat instead. The "trouble" turned out to be the day of riots in which many British institutions, including the Turf Club and the famous Shepheards Hotel, were burned to the ground. Many people, including several of our friends, were killed. Noel Thomas, headmaster of the English School, saved his own life by jumping out of the window and into a dustbin, breaking his leg in the process. One good friend of mine was disembowelled, as was her husband. David was a lecturer at Cairo University and the tragic irony is that he and Olive had been ardent supporters of the Egyptian Nationalist movement. They had been lunching at the Turf Club before catching a flight home to England.

Because he was almost part of the furniture at the club and because his body was not found, the British Embassy presumed my father dead and burnt beyond recognition. They included his name among those missing when they cabled the news home and for three anxiety-ridden days – no news was coming out of Egypt – I thought this must have been so. In fact, he had a grandstand view of the riots. As a journalist that must have been gratifying. As a human being he grieved, I know, over the anti-British feelings that had grown in his beloved Egypt. As for myself, I was enormously comforted during those anxious three days by my boyfriend and future husband, John Ormerod, who spent as much time as possible by my side.)

I noticed one day that Aunt Rosie's stomach had swollen in an alarming way and at lunchtime I asked her what was wrong. My father's fork froze in mid-air and my aunt looked embarrassed. She muttered something about constipation, but I knew this couldn't be the truth. In exasperation I didn't pursue the matter. When my father and I returned from our annual home leave in September there was a new member of the family, baby Jane. I did not make the connection.

I was enchanted by Jane. She was a pretty, blonde, merry baby and I longed to play with her, but those were the days of strict routines for babies and her nanny, Pat, had almost total care of her. Aunt Rosie fed her and prepared her for bed. I used to sit in the drawing room watching her. Like Granny Seddall with me, my aunt rocked Jane and crooned to her: not Golden Slumbers, but

> 'When Irish eyes are smiling
> Then it's like a morn in Spring.
> In the lilt of Irish laughter
> You can hear the angels sing.
> When Irish hearts are happy
> All the world is bright and gay,
> And when Irish eyes are smiling
> Sure they steal your heart away.'

I now shared my nursery with Jane and Pat. Pat was eighteen, a pretty brunette, daughter of an Army sergeant based at Abbassia, and secretly engaged to a young RAF corporal, Ray. I don't remember the reason for the secrecy. I suppose it was to do with Pat's age and maybe in the services, too, it was frowned upon to marry too young in those days. I became devoted to Pat who was like a casual but affectionate older sister to me. She spent most evenings, when Ray was not visiting her, making a trousseau. I remember watching her working on an exquisite petticoat of pink satin trimmed with lace and saying, 'I can't think why you're going to so much trouble. Ray isn't going to see you in it.' Pat blushed and offered no explanation. Another mystery!

My father and I went home every summer as usual. Sometimes we went by the long sea route. On one occasion the England Test cricket team were returning on the same boat from Australia and I got their autographs. Another summer we must have gone overland because we had a brief stay in Sicily with the Lees. Mr. Lee was my father's motoring correspondent and a teacher, his daughter, Pat, a good friend.

One more summer was to be spent with Aunt Vi in Cork, another with all the Llewellyns in a rented house in Sandbanks, when every possible moment was spent on the beach. Another memory was of driving round in Uncle Don's large open tourer, singing songs. These were the best holidays of all.

When the Llewellyns were not having summer leave in England, I would move around from one family to another. I stayed with Mollie Leggitt, who was to become a key figure in my childhood. Her husband, John, was London correspondent for *Al Ahram,* the main Egyptian daily paper, and they had two very young children, Jeannine and Romalita. They lived in a mansion flat in Hammersmith and our main excitement was to go for a walk in Ravenscourt Park. Mollie seemed rather glamorous to me. Then in her twenties, she had light auburn curly hair and brilliant blue eyes and had a blithe air about her.

I would stay with my older cousin Lena and her new husband Ian who had a flat in Hendon. They looked after me well in spite of the fact that they enjoyed teasing me. I realise now that this was probably born of envy. Lena had lost her mother when she was born. Her father had been crippled in an accident and was unable to earn a good living. My father had supported the family and had acted much as a substitute father, although absent much of the time. Then I had been born and, unlike her quite hard upbringing, I was leading a privileged life. Lena always thought I was spoiled. For my part, I didn't feel the least bit spoiled. I took for granted our Cairo life style, junketing round Europe and England, in particular London. It was interesting and enjoyable, but didn't necessarily make for happiness. By comparison the Findlaters' life was pedestrian. Ian was a bank clerk with the Hong Kong and Shanghai Bank, who later was to rise to a responsible position. For the whole of his working life he was to travel daily to the City from Hendon. Lena spent her days doing housework, shopping and walking their bad-tempered mongrel dog, which had been rescued from a circus. They had no children. Their recreation was to go to the cinema every Saturday night and to have two weeks' holiday each year in Elgin, Ian's home town. No wonder they were envious of me.

There were other families who had me to stay and it was nothing to be put in a train, in the charge of the guard, to go from one part of England to another. The guard would be tipped at the beginning of the journey and he would come and look at me from time to time. Otherwise I was in the care of the other passengers, who always seemed kindness itself. I felt no fears at all and remember feeling very humiliated on one occasion when Uncle Edgar, Uncle Don's eldest brother, pinned an identity label on my coat when he saw me off to London.

However, I did see more of my father. He stayed at the Savage Club in Adelphi Terrace, off the Strand and overlooking the Thames. It was a club for writers, artists, members of the theatrical profession and Bernard Shaw had lived in the terrace. Adelphi Terrace has now gone and the club has moved to rather grander premises on Pall Mall. I often spent the day with him in London, sometimes accompanying him on his business visits: the Egyptian Tourist Office in Piccadilly, John Leggitt's offices in Grand Buildings overlooking Trafalgar Square, Mr. Percy's advertising agency, a Dickensian office, up winding, dusty stairs into small rooms lined with shelves groaning with old files. We would eat often at my father's favourite, the White Heather Tea Rooms in the Strand, where you could get home-cooked Scots food and high teas. He took me to the theatre and to the ballet. I began to know that area of London well: Villiers Street, the Strand, Fleet Street, Piccadilly, and happily bounced my googly ball as we walked along the pavement. As the point of a googly ball was that you never knew in which direction it would land, I can only presume the traffic was negligible. I certainly remember retrieving it from the middle of the Strand.

Back in Cairo, social life still centred on the playground or the swimming baths at the Club. I have one vivid memory of walking home, hungry for lunch, my body tingling and refreshed from a morning's swimming, the sun beating down on my wet hair, the heat of the asphalt road striking the soles of my feet through my sandals. I was struck by the scent of the mimosa tree by the cricket pitch and suddenly felt a shaft of pure happiness. I would have walked on past the tennis courts, past the grounds of the Lotfallah Palace on one side, the "little palace" (as I called it) on the other. It was in fact Amer Bey's home, a pretty, pink, domed building filled with Impressionist art, had I but known it. It is now a museum. Under the banyan tree, through the little midan, past the Gezira Casino and into the cool courtyard of Gezira House. Up in the rickety lift to the cool of the flat, dark because the shutters had been closed against the sun.

Occasionally I would be invited to "play with" another child. My least favourite invitation of this sort was to Mona Abboud's. Mona's father, Abboud Pasha, was a wealthy man with vast farming estates in the Delta. He was married to a Scotswoman who was a great friend of my father's. She was apparently considered to be pretentious, perhaps because of her humble origins. But she seemed to me delightful, a twinkling, white-haired woman. She and my father would talk Scotland over tea, while Mona and I played. The trouble was that although our parents enjoyed each other's company, Mona and I heartily disliked each other.

I stayed overnight occasionally, once before one of her parties. Beforehand we went down to the kitchens in the basement to watch the preparations. To decorate the table the chef was making the most beautiful galleons and baskets of spun sugar.

The best "play with" invitations came from Patsy Lee. Her father was a teacher with P.I. (Public Instruction). Members of the P.I. were looked down upon by the British community. They were either lecturers at Cairo University or teachers in Egyptian Government schools. They were badly paid and lived in unfashionable parts of the city and would not have been members of the Club. There is the apocryphal story of the two Oxbridge graduates who met in the street.

'What are you doing out here?' asked one.

'I'm with the Embassy. And you?'

'Well, I'm with P.I., but for God's sake don't tell the family. They think I'm playing the piano in a night club.'

Nevertheless some famous people passed through the ranks of P.I., including in our time Robert Graves and Malcolm Muggeridge.

Patsy's father was another "fun" person, a blue-eyed Irishman. Like many Egyptian Government servants he sported a *tarboosh,* a variation on the Turkish *fez,* red with a black tassel, but with a deeper crown. Wearing of this headgear was later banned in Egypt except as a tourist attraction, as too reminiscent of Turkish rule. He often took us out into the desert by car and talked to us about its geological development. One of Patsy's parties was held in the desert beyond the Pyramids, when we had great fun sliding down the sand dunes. Her parties at home were hilarious affairs, with original, inventive games.

The question of religion raised its head.

My parents, being lapsed Catholics, had never taken me to church and, apart from my night prayers and a belief in God, I knew nothing of organised religion.

I had discovered I was Roman Catholic – and therefore Different – when I was at the English School in Helwan. Bertha and I were sent off to Mass every Sunday. We sat near the back of the church, unable to see the altar, unaware of the mystery being enacted there, unaffected by the candles, the music and the incense. We were bored stiff and played with our collection of money, to the accompaniment of 'tut-tutting' from the row of nuns behind us. Once a week, at school in Bulaq, we went to religious instruction given by a Franciscan Friar, but he was unable to keep order. Recognising a weak teacher when they saw one, some of the class ran riot regularly and I learnt nothing from this good man.

My non-Catholic friends tried to enlighten me:

'Being a Catholic means you'll burn in Hell if you eat meat on Friday.'

'Being a Catholic means you mustn't say 'For Thine is the Kingdom, the Power and the Glory' at the end of the Lord's Prayer.'

Baffled, I turned to Aunt Rosie for help. She was bottle-feeding Jane in the drawing room.

'Aunt Rosie, are you a Catholic?'

'No dear.'

'Why not?'

(Hesitation) 'Because I don't believe all the things that Catholics believe.'

(I struggled with the concept of belief.) 'What – like believing in fairies?'

'No dear. You'll understand when you're older.

Mystery upon mystery!

My father decided something must be done. I was nine years old and hadn't yet made my First Communion. The usual age for this for Catholic children was seven, the Jesuits' "age of reason". A friend of his offered to prepare me for this.

Lady Brand lived in the little midan near Gezira House and I started going to her flat weekly. She was an artist, married to a Squadron Leader in the RAF. They had two children called, unbelievably, Mary and Joseph. My hard heart took against these apparently model children who went to the convent school and weren't part of the hurly burly of life at the club. We had little in common and, in the event, saw little of each other.

I learnt the catechism.

'Who made you?'

'God made me.'

'Why did God make you?'

'He made me to love and serve Him in this world and to be happy with Him for ever in the next.'

And so on.

I learnt the seven deadly sins, the five cardinal virtues, the Ten Commandments and much else. Lady Brand must have interpreted the catechism, but the trick was to learn it by heart and I was a quick learner. In due course I was tested by a priest and pronounced ready for my First Communion.

It was a beautiful ceremony, which took place in the little Convent chapel in Gezira. I wore a white veil and white satin dress made by a rather boring new friend of my father's, Miss Ingle, and was the only First Communicant. The small chapel was crowded and filled with white flowers. In addition the altar rail and my pew were draped in white satin. The nuns sang sweetly and smiled at me sweetly. I felt special, a little bewildered. After mass I went back to the Brands' flat for the communion breakfast and was given presents: a prayer book, a rosary, a small statue of Our Lady. The family were unusually kind to me and yet I couldn't feel comfortable among such goodness.

And now, of course, it meant going to Mass on Sundays and this I really did resent! My father and I went into Cairo, either to St. Joseph's Cathedral – large, run by the Franciscans – or to the more intimate, atmospheric Armenian Church. And I would be missing all the fun at the swimming pool! On Sunday mornings the pool would be crowded with adults as well as us children and for some reason this added a special buzz of excitement. By the time I arrived after Mass half the morning had gone.

Then there was the question of my education.

Madame Morin's was a happy, sunny school, but small and undemanding. There were only about a hundred pupils, a third of whom were English. I was in a class of about ten children, ranging in age from eight to ten years old. Our form teacher was a gentle young woman whose homesickness for England manifested itself in our introduction to such poems as "Oh, to be in England" and "To daffodils", although few of us would have seen a daffodil or experienced the glories of an English spring.

The school was strong on the arts and one term a dance drama was planned for the school display. I was given the star part of the god Pan. I was to make my entrance from behind a temple pillar and then dance daintily round the stage, playing my pipes. When the great day came I, unfortunately, forgot to take off my plimsolls, so I emerged from the pillar, not a vision of grace, but an embarrassed child (I immediately realised what I had done) clumping about in white shoes to the accompaniment of hisses from the Misses Simpson, the dancing teachers. That is a bad memory, but otherwise I was very happy there.

I was warned that I would be going to boarding school in England but this presented no threat. Three schoolgirl magazines had recently come on the market: *Schoolgirl, Schoolgirl's Own* and *Schoolgirl Weekly*. We fed on these and acted out the parts of the girls who featured regularly in the stories. Elsie Vernon Jarvis, our natural leader, was Babs Redfern, leader of the school gang, Gamila Green, a dark Jewess, played the part of an Indian princess, I was the pretty but dim Paula. I can't remember who played the part of the hapless Bessie Bunter, Billy's sister. Their adventures were so romantic and exciting that we firmly believed that English boarding schools would offer similar delights.

I have two snapshot memories of Nanny at this time, so she must have returned to look after me although I can't remember when or why. Nor do I have any other such memories.

The first memory is of the two of us in a box at the Cairo Opera House watching Sybil Thorndike in the sleepwalking scene from *Macbeth*. It is a vivid memory: the sight of Lady Macbeth in a long white gown, hair falling down her back, distressingly rubbing her hands. Robert Atkins brought his company out to Cairo each winter in the Thirties and my father became friendly with them all. I had already seen *The Admirable Crichton* and been taken backstage afterwards and I had cajoled my father into letting me see *Macbeth*. I was determined to get my way and, against his better judgement, he permitted it. We also went to see the company in Regents Park one summer and I remember how disillusioned I had been after that visit backstage. I had been totally absorbed in *A Midsummer Night's Dream* and was startled afterwards when Titania turned out to be a large painted lady welcoming us with "Darlings!"

The second snapshot memory is of Nanny sitting by my bed, applying cold compresses to my forehead. I had a high fever and it must have been after this that I was admitted to the Anglo-American Hospital with paratyphoid. I was in hospital for a month with a recurrent temperature and no treatment apart from total bed-rest and a fluid diet. I was allowed barley sugar, which was put by my bed, long curly sticks of it in a jar, which in turn stood in a bowl of water. I would watch the ants crawling up the side of the bowl and then drowning in their attempt to get at the sugar.

No visitors were allowed because of the risk of infection until my temperature went down, which it stubbornly refused to do however well I felt. I read all the children's books in the hospital library and was further sustained by copies of the Schoolgirl weeklies sent to me by "Aunty Carty", a family friend. In the end I resorted to writing my own schoolgirl novel, a copy of which I still have. The only visitor towards the end, apart from my father, was faithful Patsy Lee. I felt very trendy when she left calling out 'Toodleoo!' to which I replied 'Pip! Pip!' Pure Wodehouse.

When I returned to the playground, thinner and taller, there were two new girls who were held in some awe because of their acrobatic prowess. It was said that they could beat any boy in a fight. They were Joan and Jessica, daughters of Air Force officers. Jo was a slim, graceful attractive girl; Jay was stronger, tougher, with an arm which had been badly set after a fracture and whose elbow stuck out at an awkward angle. They included me in their friendship, christened me Pumpkin for some unknown reason and soon taught me the secrets of their acrobatics.

We all three went to Madame Morin's and used to walk home from school together. We would then go to one or another for tea. Their mothers and my aunt never worried if we didn't come home: we were obviously having tea in one of the three flats.

It didn't take us long to realise that we didn't have to go home at all after school. No questions would be asked. We began to have a street life of our own. We played the good old trick of going to the top of a block of flats and ringing all the doorbells as we raced down the stairs. We invaded building sites, daring one another to walk across planks precariously balanced up high. We jumped on to the backs of donkey carts, making their way to market in Cairo, jumping off again as they reached Bulaq Bridge. (There were certain risks we would not take and one of them was to go into Bulaq.) I even remember Jay having a hand-to-hand fight with the *boab* of Jo's block of flats.

We were found out of course and a crisis was reached when it was discovered that one of the servants in Jay's block of flats had exposed himself to us. Our street life came to an end and the servant lost his *tahteeb* (work permit) and probably had to return to his village. The servant was not taken to court – "it would take for ever" – but I was struck by the enormity of the punishment he did receive and for some time felt guilty about it.

Jo and Jay were now considered to be a bad example to me and I was forbidden to play with them. This was not so hard to bear, because we still met at school and the swimming pool and in any case I was soon due to go home to England to boarding school.

I looked forward to this change and was the envy of my friends who were staying on in Cairo. On the day before we sailed, my father took me to the club to make my farewells and as we looked into the tea gardens for friends I felt unutterably sad. I felt I might never come back.

As a ten-year-old what impressions did I take away of Egypt? How much did I understand of this complex fascinating country?

. . . I knew it was home. England was all very well, but Egypt was where I belonged. England was peaceful, quiet, safe, welcoming, but on the whole rather bland. When we landed at Port Said or Alexandria, and the smells of spices and garlic rose from the quayside, as the shouting street vendors jostled for attention and the heat beat down on us, I would feel an excited recognition and know that I was home.

. . . I realised that there was great wealth and immense poverty among the Egyptians. I knew them to be a gentle and courteous people with a quick sense of humour. But I had also witnessed sudden violent outbreaks of street fighting. I knew they could fast from dawn to dusk for a month during *Ramadan* and feast during the night. Just as they could dance and sing in joyous abandon at the feast of *Bairam,* the young girls dressed in El Greco colours of saffron yellow, emerald green, candy pink. The staple diet of the working classes was *fool* (beans) which my father and I loved, but which cook would only reluctantly supply as being unworthy of an English table. I knew servants to be silent and obsequious, but that the street cafés were always full of gesticulating, argumentative men. (Planning our downfall, probably, had I but realised it.)

. . . I expected each morning to wake to a clear blue sky and a sun-filled day. There was rain about once a year. Also once a year we would be assailed by *khamseens* (desert winds). The most common one was an oppressive wind that sapped one's energy so that one could hardly breathe or move. Almost worse was the wind that blew sand into Cairo from the desert, so that one's face and arms and eyes stung painfully. Then one was kept home from school and all windows and shutters were tightly closed.

. . . My knowledge of Cairo was limited mainly to Gezira and its leafy avenues. However, I was familiar with the important thoroughfare of Sharia Fuad el Awal (Fuad the First Street – now Sharia July 26) which runs through the island from Bulaq Bridge and links central Cairo eventually with the Pyramids. It would finally run in a straight line from Gizeh through the wide fields of the Delta to the Pyramids. Now the Pyramids Road is hideously built up. Then one could see the tiny triangles of the Pyramids on the horizon and watch them gradually grow until they towered above one. Uncle Don used to say this was most impressive by moonlight. Sharia Fuad el Awal was always busy, the trams clanking noisily by, hooting cars, donkeys laden with *berseem,* camels walking in caravan laden with market produce.

. . . My knowledge of central Cairo was mainly limited to visits to my father's office and the famous Shepheard's Hotel, where we were on close friendly terms with Charles Muller, the Swiss manager, and his family. I visited the Vernon Jarvis girls in their Cairo flat. Their father was an officer in the Egyptian Police, their mother Italian, a sweet welcoming figure. I had my hair cut at Maison Georges, in early years sitting on a wooden painted horse. Other visits were made to the dentist. I only once went to the *muski* bazaar with the wife of Robert Atkins' stage manager. I was not to get to know the streets of Cairo until my teens.

. . . I knew nothing of the political situation and the strong Nationalist movement. There was a King Fuad and a royal court and an Egyptian parliament, but it seemed to me that we, the British, ran everything. The Anglo-Egyptian Treaty of 1933 had just been signed, whereby more autonomy was to be given to the Egyptians. The main difference for the English was that as they died or retired from the Civil Service so their jobs would be taken over by Egyptians. In return, we could keep our military, air and naval bases and would defend Egypt (and the Suez Canal of course) in the event of war.

... and a New Beginning

My father, when he was on holiday, assumed a new personality. As soon as we were on our way he visibly relaxed, seemed to dismiss the cares and worries of everyday life and became a delightful, entertaining and thoughtful companion.

For this last holiday before I went to boarding school we were to have three weeks in Venice, followed by a stay on Lake Lucerne. We were to stay in two top class hotels in return for a series of advertisements in *The Sphinx*. 'A palace in Italy and a castle in Switzerland!' my father chuckled. He more than once expressed amused delight at the lifestyle he enjoyed when his early life had been spent in Aberdeen, the son of an impoverished widowed teacher. I hope that he also congratulated himself on the fact that this was largely due to his own talents and capacity for hard work.

In the event we had our time in Venice, but for some reason the Lucerne stay was cancelled. We stayed at the Gritti Palace on the Grand Canal. It was then the best hotel in Venice, an opulent, cavernous place. We befriended two American men and did the sights with them.

One memorable evening there was a *fiesta* on the Grand Lagoon and we took a gondola out to join in. The lagoon was crowded with gondolas carrying coloured Chinese lanterns. The sound of *gondolieri* singing in their lovely tenor voices drifted across the water. It was magical.

Barbara Hutton, the Woolworth's heiress, came to the Gritti Palace on her (first) honeymoon. At that time she was as well known as Princess Diana was to become. Like Diana she was beautiful and slim and reputed to be the richest heiress in the world. She was to marry several times and died a lonely unhappy woman, but in 1933 we couldn't have foreseen that and her marriage to the Georgian Prince Alexis

Mdivani had all the necessary elements for a fairy tale romance. We four were given a private view of the honeymoon suite. It came straight out of a Hollywood musical: banks of flowers, and the four-poster bed was made up with silken sheets, hand-embroidered with the Prince's crest.

We four took up a strategic position on the hotel terrace for their arrival. In spite of their fame there was not one single photographer; the paparazzi had not yet been invented and in any case there was no need for them. No television and scarcely any picture magazines. We had a perfect view as they arrived by gondola. Barbara Hutton walked past with her eyes downcast, but the handsome dark prince gave me a smile that I still remember. They were followed by six gondolas of luggage, a fact that we noted with awe.

The rest of that summer holiday was spent by me with the Llewellyns in Sandbanks in Dorset, until towards the end my father took me to stay with some friends in Cambridge, the Dennis Jones.

The Reverend Dennis Jones was Precentor at Trinity College Chapel and a composer in a small way of sacred music. He and my father had shared a tent in Palestine during the Great War and had evidently remained good friends, although I had never heard of him before, He was now in his forties, a large, benevolent, scholarly man, married to a vivacious red-haired wife in her twenties, Merle. They had two children, Robin, four, and Christine, two, and lived in a large rambling Victorian house in Grange Road, opposite Newnham College.

My father was due to return to Egypt in a fortnight and so far no decision seemed to have been made about my schooling. If it had been, as was customary at the time, I had not been consulted or informed. I got the impression that my father had not given the matter serious consideration and began to wonder if I would return to Cairo after all. Maybe he had been making enquiries for months. I don't know.

Mr. Dennis Jones could highly recommend that I should go to St. Mary's Convent in Cambridge. He was friendly with the Reverend Mother, who had been converted from Anglicanism and with whom he often met for theological discussion. The school's academic record was good, the boarding school itself was small, the Dennis Jones could keep an eye on me in my father's absence. Altogether it seemed a good choice.

We went to the convent for an interview and I was accepted. Within a few days I was installed at school, before term started, and my father was on his way home to Egypt.

It was one of the wisest choices he could have made for me.

'Studies serve for delight,
for ornament and for ability'
Francis Bacon. Essays

CONVENT GIRL
1933-39

The New Boarder*

I have to disappoint you by reporting that this is not going to be another tale of cruel, blinkered nuns and wretched children. I was at the Convent from the ages of ten to sixteen and was extremely happy there.

On the way to our interview I was nervous. I had never been inside a convent nor spoken to a nun before – apart from Great Aunt Mary, my father's aunt, who was stone deaf and had terrified me with her loud voice and ear trumpet. Our introduction to the convent was not promising. My father and I found ourselves outside stout green gates set in a high thick wall. Inside a drive led up to a large double-fronted house, draped with wisteria, everywhere silent and unmoving. But then the door was opened by the broadly smiling Sister Boniface, the porteress. I felt better.

We were ushered into the Parlour to the right of the front door: a small formal room which looked out on the garden. Through the tall windows I could see a lawn with lily pond and fountain in the middle, a cedar tree to one side, shrubberies to the other and at the far end of the lawn a tennis court, beyond which were more shrubberies. After a while we were joined by Mr Dennis Jones' friend, Reverend Mother Anselm. She was a quiet, gentle woman, who was only to be our Reverend Mother for the next year.

After the usual formalities, Sister Cecilia came in. She was headmistress of the boarding house and was academically and pastorally responsible for the boarders. At that time the boarding and day-schools were strictly segregated. They even occupied different sites, divided by a strip of the Botanical Gardens. For my first year I was to be barely aware of the day-school's existence.

* The names of all the nuns and lay teaching staff at the Convent have been changed.

Sister Cecilia took me for a walk round the garden and before we were halfway round I realised that here was someone with whom I felt completely at ease. I think I did all the talking, she encouraged me, seemed amused and appreciative of my stories and comments. She was in fact to have the most profound effect on me, as she must have done on many of us, for she entered so completely into our lives and interests.

When we returned to the parlour and my father had presumably told Mother Anselm of my mother's defection in privacy, it was agreed that I should move in to the convent as soon as possible. Within a few days, before the start of term, I was installed and my father had left for Egypt. No mention of my mother was made then or indeed for some time.

There were very few boarders at Cambridge – at most about twenty – and one year, when the Depression had done its worst, we were down to nine. There were no dormitories. We all slept in rooms of two or three girls, and for my first year I was to share a room with Veronica Jones, even younger than me, and with Sister Cecilia. The latter slept behind a curtain in the corner of the room. We never heard her rise in the morning or go to bed at night, but it was nevertheless comforting to know that she was there while we were asleep. The other nuns had their own rooms (cells) in their half of the house.

Sister Cecilia took charge of preparing me for the coming term. We went shopping for suitable clothes in the town. There was no uniform, except that for games and gym we wore gymslips, long black stockings and black bloomers (with white cotton liners). The only stipulation otherwise was that we should wear blue and most of us wore navy skirts and blue tops in winter, blue dresses (any pattern and design) in summer. Navy hats in winter, straw hats (a new statutory design, stylish) each summer. But winter underwear also had to be bought and those were the days of liberty bodices. The one thing they did not give was liberty. They were made of thick cotton, constrained with thick vertical strips of (?) calico, (?) linen. They covered one's body and had suspenders at the bottom to hold up one's thick lisle stockings.

Sister also showed me round the house. The "School" in which lessons were taught to most of the girls and where we did our homework, was on the ground floor, with an anteroom off it. Also on the ground floor were the large dining room and the cloakroom. A sweeping staircase led to the first floor where we had the "Study", the room in which we had our recreation and where the library was kept. Along the corridor was Reverend Mother's office. The rest of the first floor was given over to bedrooms and bathrooms. Some bedrooms had a piano in them and homework time would be accompanied by girls practising above our heads. On the top floor there were more bedrooms and bathrooms, but at the head of the staircase were the pretty little chapel and the sacristy. The nuns lived in another wing of the house.

I was introduced to Sister Cecilia's "shop": a glass cupboard filled with prayer books, missals, crucifixes, statues and holy pictures. I bought my first rosary and my missal, which I loved with its petal-thin paper, gold leaf edges and charming illustrations. I still have it. She also reminded me how to take communion, as I had not done so since my First Communion.

A few days after I had moved in, the front doors opened and in poured my new companions.

For the most part, they were rather intimidating: large, self-confident and sophisticated. I felt young and naïve by comparison. There were the Humphries sisters who talked of "doing the season" when they left school. There was also talk by others of the finishing school in Munich that elder sisters had been to and that they were destined for. There was the head girl, cool and sophisticated, of whom we were all envious because on doctor's orders she had a banana and cream every morning for breakfast.

Veronica, who shared my room, was a beautiful, delicate child with an unusual talent as a pianist. Unfortunately she believed in fairies and ghosts and so tended to be teased. Her parents removed her at the end of the year, but for a while we were companions.

Veronica and I were to have our lessons in the anteroom off the School, together with two girls called Bunty and Mary. Bunty was the daughter of an Indian Army colonel and only saw her parents every few years when they came home on leave. Her holidays were spent with her grandmother. She was a large uncoordinated girl, with tip-tilted nose and innocent blue eyes. Mary was congenitally deformed. She had virtually no ears and was hard of hearing. She also had a cleft palate, so her speech tended to be indistinct. Her face was unformed and ugly, but she had a gentle, sweet temperament and a delightful Irish sense of humour.

Our lessons in the anteroom were easy compared to the rigorous standards I had come to expect in Egypt. I began to be slightly bored by the lessons. Everything was to change for me in the following September, when I would start lessons at the day-school, but I didn't know this.

One would have thought that the biggest adjustment would have been to the religious ambience that pervaded each day. In fact, I took to it like the proverbial duck.

The day was punctuated by bells and prayers. Bells for chapel, bells for lessons, prayers throughout the day.

We would be woken by Sister Cecilia doing the rounds: *Benedicamus Domino* (Let us praise the Lord), to which we would reply *Deo Gratias* (Thanks be to God). When we were dressed, we went either to Mass at 7.15 or to morning prayers when Mass was over. (The younger one was, the less often one was expected to go to weekday Mass. My first year I went once a week, but when I was in the Sixth Form I had only one "long sleep" a week. Oh, the bliss of hearing Sister Cecilia pass by one's room and know one had an extra half-hour in bed!)

Breakfast was preceded and followed by grace. Prayers before morning and afternoon classes. And everything stopped for the Angelus at midday and at six in the evening:

V.   The angel of the Lord declared unto Mary.
R.   And she conceived of the Holy Ghost.

Hail Mary, full of grace, the Lord is with thee; blessed art thou among women and blessed is the fruit of they womb, Jesus.

Holy Mary, Mother of God, pray for us sinners, now and at the hour of our death.

V.   Behold the handmaid of the Lord:
R.   Be it done unto me according to Thy word.

Hail Mary . . .

V.   And the Word was made flesh.
R.   And dwelt amongst us.

Hail Mary . . .

The day ended with night prayers in the chapel.

At the weekend there was Confession in the parish church on Saturday. Always a problem to find enough sins to justify this excursion. Lies and sins against charity were always a safe bet. On Sunday of course there was obligatory Mass in the chapel when we wore white veils (black veils on weekdays) and at least once a month one had to go to High Mass at the parish church as well. The convent girls occupied the front row in church where some of us took a healthy interest in the boys in the choir. In retrospect the latter were a pretty unappealing selection, but they wore trousers and were the best option available. Also being in the front row meant that we were observed by the eagle eyes of the "Catholic Cats". These good members of the Catholic Women's League, who had been christened the Catholic Cats by a previous generation of Convent girls, periodically complained about our behaviour – the way we genuflected or the whispering during the service or *something*. We heartily disliked them. (When I was to tell my mother about them she said, 'Ah yes, *les punaises de sacristie,* French priests call them: Sacristy bugs, always hanging about the priest's skirts.' Yet I now realise no parish would survive without these hard-working women.)

Also on Sunday there was Benediction (reveration of the Host which was displayed in a golden-rayed monstrance): Benediction in the chapel or at the parish church.

Once a year we went into a weekend retreat – silence from Friday evening to Sunday evening – which was usually taken by a Jesuit. He gave two or three addresses a day and one could see him privately if one wanted. Otherwise it was time for prayer, contemplation and the reading of improving books.

There was also weekly "spidge" (said with one's thumb turned down). This was Spiritual Reading when we darned our newly returned laundry, while one of the nuns read to us, usually from the life of a saint.

I learnt how to make the Catholic devotions of the Stations of the Cross and the Rosary.

The Stations are to be found in every Catholic church and chapel. They are twelve pictures or sculptures of scenes from Christ's Passion. (There are some fine ones by Eric Gill in Westminster Cathedral.) The devotion is to pause at each, contemplate the scene and say a prayer. This was a favourite devotion in Lent.

The rosary was said frequently, either aloud with others or by oneself. Here there were three groups of "mysteries": Joyful (connected with Christ's birth and childhood), Sorrowful (His passion) and Glorious (His resurrection and ascension to Heaven). In each group there were five scenes to contemplate while one said ten Hail Marys, preceded by an Our Father and followed by a Glory Be. These devotions introduced us to contemplative prayer.

Then there were novenas. These were supplications to Our Lady or a saint whereby one had to say the same prayer for nine days running.

Religion informed much of our everyday conversation. This must sound insufferably pious, but – and it is hard to explain this to a non-Catholic – we also wore our religion lightly. We could not understand converts to Catholicism who took their religion seriously and without humour and felt uneasy with Mother Anselm's earnest approach. Although some of us had Anglican fathers, we considered Anglicans to be misguided heretics, whose services were occasions that it was considered socially desirable to attend. In short, our understanding of religion was inevitably childish. We are also talking of the days before Vatican Two and the ecumenical movement.

I don't think we were arrogant – just self-assured. We were members of the true church, a worldwide family descended from Christ's apostles, with an earthly father, the Pope, and a father in Heaven, surrounded by angels and saints, all of whom were rooting for us!

Schools are much the same in any place and in any age. The Convent was unusual in being so small, so that we could get individual attention and there was no strong academic pressure. Traditional lessons took place in the mornings, but in the afternoons we had art, sport, gym or needlework, etc. On Monday afternoons Sister Cecilia took us for a walk, either in the Botanical Gardens next door or round one of the colleges or to the Fitzwilliam Museum. The balance between lessons, sport and the arts was well kept, as it was at the day-school.

Some memories of our Convent life . . .

. . . "Canon Youens", named after the Canon who had founded a nearby Catholic orphanage. This was an afternoon each term when we devised our own competitions and side shows to raise money for the orphans. In the evening we put on a play: Noel Coward's *Cavalcade* my first term when I played the part of a small child.

. . . Sister Cecilia's feast day each November when a fire was lit in the Study and we roasted chestnuts while she read us ghost stories. She enjoyed reading aloud to us and we were over the years introduced to *The Woman in White* and *The Mysteries of Udolpho* among others. She loved the Gothic novels.

. . . May Week (a fortnight in June) when we joined in as many of the university's junketings as possible: going to Fenners to watch the tennis championships; going to the "bumps" when all the college rowing teams attempted to bump the boat in front; madrigals on the river. (There is a story about the madrigals worth the telling, partly because it caused a minor stir at the time, partly because it illustrates How Times Have Changed! The singers sang from a row of punts tethered together by Clare Bridge. As darkness fell they would move off down the river singing *Draw on Sweet Night*.

End of recital. This was an annual ritual and the recital a regular part of the BBC's summer programme. One year a ripple of laughter followed the punts. As they passed us we could see that some schoolboyish undergraduates had stolen chamber pots from Clare College, lit candles in them and tied them to the back of the punts. The recital was broadcast live and the nuns had been listening. When we got home to hot chocolate, Sister Cecilia asked about the laughter. The head girl drew her aside to explain. Sister was amused, but not so Lord Reith and Auntie BBC. An announcement was made that the madrigals would not be broadcast again.)

. . . "Corpus Christi". Every summer term, when the Feast of Corpus Christi fell, a local old Catholic family who lived in Sawston Hall held an open-air Benediction in the grounds of their stately home. This was attended by hundreds of Catholics from the surrounding area. The proceedings started with a procession round the magnificent grounds, singing hymns, followed by Benediction and a short sermon by the Bishop. It was an event that was highly charged emotionally, the more so for us Convent girls because afterwards a special tea – plates of éclairs and cream buns – was served for us in the great hall. Then we piled into a coach and sang all the way home.

. . . Laburnum Woods. We were often taken for long walks in the country and a favourite excursion, again in the summer term, was a picnic lunch at Laburnum Woods. After eating, we were free to roam the countryside as long as we were back in time for the return journey. We would split off into twos or threes and as far as I know nobody ever came to any harm.

. . . Nursery tea with the Dennis Jones: a roaring fire behind the large fireguard, fat nanny presiding over the table. Every Saturday of my first year I would walk along Fen Causeway and Grange Road to spend the day with the Dennis Jones: lunch with Mr and Mrs Dennis Jones, afternoon walk followed by tea with Robin and Christine. Robin was a serious, quiet little boy, Christine blonde, blue-eyed and bubbly. Tea always included chocolate finger biscuits and iced biscuits with nursery rhyme pictures on them. But we couldn't have them until we'd eaten our bread and butter first. Over the years these Saturday visits dwindled to two or three a term. (Many, many years later I was to renew my friendship with Robin, and he was to become godfather to one of my sons.)

. . . "Bug-hunting". Vulgar, schoolgirl term for a weekly ritual. Every Saturday morning a nun would comb one's hair with a fine-tooth comb, inspect one's nails and check one's room was tidy. I can't imagine this procedure lasted long after I left.

. . . Dancing classes. Every Thursday evening we filed round to the day-school where we were taught ballroom dancing and, one term, tap-dancing. On one occasion our teacher taught us the latest trendy dance. The Sister who was escorting us asked if this was strictly necessary. 'Oh, but the girls must be able to dance it at their Christmas dances,' replied the teacher. There was absolutely no hope of any of us going to "Christmas dances", but we preened self-consciously and continued the class.

. . . June 29. My birthday and also the Feast of SS. Peter and Paul. Therefore the feast day of both myself and Mother Peter, who had succeeded Mother Anselm as Reverend Mother and who was Headmistress of the day-school. But also on this day we held the day-school's garden fete in the Convent garden. A day off, sideshows, teas, a play by the Lower VI – and all on my birthday!

. . . My father had given blanket approval to my going to any concerts or plays that the nuns thought suitable and over my years at Cambridge I went to some wonderful performances. The highlight in my memory was the *B Minor*

Mass in King's College Chapel, lit by a blaze of candles. (I learnt only recently that David Greenham, who was to marry cousin Marian, was one of the undergraduates singing in that performance.)

My first summer term, my father came home to England earlier than usual, partly in order to have an operation on his hand in a Cambridge nursing home. After school, I would visit him at the home, walking along the Trumpington Road, past the Botanical Gardens. We had long talks on these visits and got to know one another even better. When he left the nursing home, he stayed for a while with the Dennis Jones and we would wander round the colleges or along the Backs. This new-found intimacy was not to last very long.

Paston House

In September, 1934, when we returned from the summer holidays, there was evidence of a new order as soon as we entered the front door. The Convent had been re-decorated and the entrance hall had a new daring wallpaper which simultaneously added dignity and a sense of space. The food at the Convent also improved dramatically.

Mother Anselm had been succeeded by Mother Peter as Reverend Mother. Mother Peter had already made her mark as headmistress of Paston House, the day-school. From being a small school she had developed it into a large school of 300 girls which was beginning to rival the Perse High School for Girls academically, while being cheaper. New classrooms had been built and Mother Peter's passion for music and drama was reflected in the curriculum.

The community of nuns, over which she now reigned, consisted of about fifteen teaching nuns and the same number of lay nuns who were responsible for all the cleaning, cooking and laundry. They wore long heavy black habits with black veils and white wimples. Round their waist was a broad black girdle from which hung a large heavy rosary. The difference in dress was that the teachers had wimples with pie-crust edges. The lay nuns' wimples were plain. They must have had lessons in deportment because they seemed to glide along, and out in the street walked with eyes downcast: the "custody of the eyes" according to former nun Karen Armstrong. (There is the true story told to me about the children at the school for the deaf who, introduced to a Catholic nun for the first time, thought she moved on wheels!)

Reverend Mother Peter was a formidable woman. Small and stout with bright blue eyes in a highly-coloured face, she resembled a good-natured Queen Victoria in nun's habit. I never felt at ease in her presence. When she fixed me with those amused blue eyes I felt sure she could read my innermost thoughts and knew of my latest misdemeanours.

Nevertheless, she was an excellent headmistress and I was now to benefit from this. Wisely, she had left Sister Cecilia still headmistress of the boarding school and there were few changes at the Convent. But it was decided that a new boarder, Dicta, and I should in future have all our lessons at Paston House. My father had been consulted and it was implied that Dicta and I were the first of a new breed of boarder who would eventually need, or choose, to work for our livings and not just make a good marriage. We therefore needed to be properly educated and not drift along in the easy-going ways of the Convent. Shortly after I left Cambridge, all the boarders and day-girls were being taught together.

I went into Form III, younger by two years than any of the other children, except for Marjorie Stearn, a year older than me and who was to accompany me through to the Sixth Form. At last the lessons stretched me and I settled down quickly. The day girls viewed me at first with caution. They had believed that all the boarders were destined to become nuns and were astonished to hear otherwise – particularly amazed to hear that we listened avidly to Radio Luxembourg (the first commercial radio station, which played the dance music of the time) and knew the latest jazz and Astaire-Rogers hits. Marjorie Stearn was pointed out to me as someone very special because she had been both to Egypt and Venice. I pondered on this fact and decided for the time being to keep quiet about my background. Marjorie's father had apparently been in Cairo as a teacher with the Egyptian Government and a holiday had been spent in Venice. This was exotic by the standards of the time. Children only went abroad if their father were serving in some part of the Empire and then they would probably be sent home to boarding school. Only the rich could afford tourism abroad, even tourism in Europe.

The next five years were spent balancing my Convent life with my day-school life. They were very different. The Convent was free and easy, but inward-looking, and most girls came from privileged backgrounds. At Paston I was meeting the daughters of Cambridge businessmen and tradesmen. I was to be more in touch with the real world outside the more closeted, cosseted world of the Convent.

Most of the girls at Paston were non-Catholic and it was interesting to see how carefully the nuns avoided any accusation that there might have been that they were in the business of conversion. Apart from Assembly in the morning there were no more prayers. As a boarder I never attended Assembly, but I understand that one of the rules given out then was 'Religion will not be discussed in the school.' Am not sure how the tricky subjects of the Middle Ages and the Tudor persecutions were handled, because by Form III we had moved on to the calmer waters of the Eighteenth century. As for religion, the Catholics had times set aside for religious instruction. Otherwise we were taught the Old Testament stories and when it came to the New Testament, in order to take School Certificate (GCSE equivalent), we learnt the gospels by heart. The Acts of the Apostles were treated as an exciting adventure story, Sister James filling in the political, economic and geographic backgrounds. It was clever and it was the right thing to do.

The order to which the nuns belonged, the Institute of the Blessed Virgin Mary, or the IBVM, had been founded in the Seventeenth Century, at the height of the Protestant persecution of the Catholics, by Mary Ward, a high-spirited Yorkshire girl of good family. She was the first woman who wished to found an order of sisters who would not remain enclosed in their convent. Following the Jesuits' "rule of St. Ignatius" she wanted them to be "with and among the people" going "where the need was greatest". She and her small band of "wandering women" started with teaching, particularly the teaching of girls, the neglect of which was one of the scandals of the time.

She had to go to the Continent to achieve this and she succeeded against the most appalling odds (including a 1,500 mile walk to Rome to plead with Pope Gregory XV to recognise her order and her later imprisonment by his successor, Urban VIII, who disbanded the sisterhood).

Eventually she founded a house in Munich. By the time I went to Cambridge there were numerous IBVM schools on the Continent, our school in Cambridge and schools in York, Hampstead, Ascot and Shaftesbury. The IBVM were and still remain in the forefront of educational theory and practice. The schools still flourish, but they have ceased to be "convents" and are no longer under the jurisdiction of the Sisters, for they have been transferred to diocesan or lay management. York is now a large diocesan comprehensive and the four independent schools in Cambridge, Ascot, Hampstead and Shaftesbury are now governed by lay trusts, each under the name of St. Mary's School.

My memories of Paston are confused, the most vivid ones being of our two years in the Sixth Form. I do remember our enjoyable introduction to Shakespeare in the Fourth Form, when we read several abridged plays on the trot, without undue interpretation and sometimes reading the parts: *Julius Caesar, The Merchant of Venice, As You Like it, Twelfth Night* and more. So when we got to the serious business of studying *Henry V* for School Certificate we were prepared to enjoy it.

Still more did we enjoy the constant diet of active drama. The School Play on Prize Day at the end of the Michaelmas term was the big event of the year. In the Lent term we held inter-house competitions in music, drama and sport. In the Summer term the Sixth Form put on an extract from the Higher Certificate Shakespeare they were studying. Mother Peter took an active interest in the drama and music, often attending rehearsals. She wanted every child to have a chance to act, just as she insisted on every child singing in the choir.

We were spoilt. Doctor Middleton, organist and choir-master at Trinity College Chapel, came regularly to coach the singing. For the school play we were visited by a retired actress, a charactered lady who would turn up, heavily painted, in an ancient leopard-skin coat and a felt Robin Hood-style hat. When I played Feste she coached me in the prison scene to imitate a deep-voiced parson. In addition, towards the end of rehearsals Roy Newlands descended upon us from London. Roy Newlands was an actor, who would sweep in accompanied by a strong scent. We used to speculate as to who was wearing the scent for these special occasions.

I enjoyed being a pupil at Paston. Apart from the sciences and art – which were badly taught at that time – I enjoyed the lessons and it was refreshing to be in touch with the outside world through the other girls. I remember few of these, oddly enough. The ones who stand out are Marjorie Stearn; Mary Howitt, a gentle Catholic whose parents let rooms to under-graduates; and Mary Reynolds, my particular friend, whose widowed mother had become housekeeper to a wealthy invalid and was now married to him. I used to go to tea with Mary, who lived in a large impressive house. A different drawing room was used every week so that each room could get thoroughly spring-cleaned. When one saw all the ornaments that filled the rooms one could understand the problem.

We four were the only ones to move up to the Sixth Form after School Certificate. The others would have taken secretarial courses or gone straight into jobs. There was no hope in those days for further training unless parents had money and to spare. The nuns grieved that one girl who was a particularly talented pianist would probably at best get a job in a piano salesroom, demonstrating the pianos. There would also be no future training for another, who had a beautiful soprano voice, but I was pleased one night, many years later, in the Bury St. Edmunds Theatre to hear her taking a leading role in a Gilbert and Sullivan opera with the D'Oyley Carte. I also remember Mary Reynolds' cousin, Helen Burleigh, who epitomised for me everything I most admired in an English girl. She was blonde, blue-eyed, amusing and intelligent with a frank, open face and manner. She made a lovely Viola in *Twelfth Night.*

Twelfth Night! It stands out as one of the most memorable days in my school life. We were in the Lower Sixth so had no examination pressures to worry about. I was Feste, Mary was Sir Toby Belch, Marjorie was Andrew Aguecheek, retiring Mary Howitt had a small part. Roy Newlands had pulled the production together and we all felt it was good. At the afternoon prize-giving I had received the Maths prize *(Jane Eyre)* and a prize for passing School Certificate *(Pride and Prejudice)* and my mother was making her one and only visit to Cambridge. (Yes, we were in touch again.) She came to the matinee and we had tea afterwards in Dorothy's in Cambridge. The evening performance, attended by the Leggitts, went so well that all I wanted to do was make my career on the stage, but I knew without asking that my father would not agree.

The next day Sister Cecilia made one of her typical gestures. Judging that I would be both emotionally and physically exhausted by the events of Prize Day – the prize-giving, my mother's visit, the performances – she came into my room early and decreed a day in bed, with meals brought to my room. She then borrowed Angela Giles' radio (she was the only girl to own one) and I spent a blissful day in bed listening to jazz and Bing Crosby and reading *Pride and Prejudice* from cover to cover.

She made many such gestures. Two or three times during School Certificate year I had woken in the morning and burst into tears. The dispensarian who was also responsible for our material needs, had no patience with this, but she was countermanded by Sister Cecilia who reckoned I was feeling the strain of the academic work and recommended a day in bed. The most amusing and imaginative gesture I remember was one summer evening when I was sharing a room with my best friend, Bee Travis. Sister came in to say goodnight as usual. Bee sighed, 'How I would love some scrambled eggs!' Ten minutes later Sister Cecilia appeared with a tray of scrambled eggs that she must have made herself.

It would be easy to write about Sister Cecilia as though she were the only teacher worth remembering, and there is no doubt she stands out in my memory above all the others. She had, in fact, been a boarder at the Convent herself. It was said that she came of a "good" Anglo-Irish family, had "done the Season" as a deb and been presented at court. But after the year of parties and balls and Ascot and Henley had decided that the life of a nun was for her. At some stage after her profession she had taken an English degree. Perhaps because she had never severed her links in her heart with the Convent, she empathised with us so well. She could talk our schoolgirl slang without sounding ridiculous and she had an infectious sense of humour. She appeared to be a woman with strong passions, whether it be for her subject of Eng. Lit. or for more personal concerns.

But of course there were other nuns who played smaller or larger parts in our lives. Mother Martha, called Mother in deference to her great age. She seemed ancient, tall and stooping, with poor sight and going deaf, but she taught me the piano with flair and enthusiasm. Sister Gertrude, who we felt had "missed her vocation" and should never have been a nun. In fact the truth was probably that she was not suited to being a teacher of young children (she was more an academic). We knew, as children do, how to play her up. There was Sister Raphael, another elderly nun who had a testy manner, but of whom we were fond. She was retired from teaching, but sometimes supervised homework at the Convent. Sister Teresa, a young, sweet, newly-professed nun who had taken most of our lessons when I was in the ante-room at the Convent. Sister Thomas, who took one of the younger forms at Paston, a brisk, friendly woman. Sister Francis, universally loved. She took the Kindergarten at Paston and was also sacristan at the Convent chapel. She always seemed deeply happy. Sister James who taught us maths and the New Testament, a quiet nun with a pale transparent look but a will of steel. These are the only teaching nuns I remember, although there must have been more. We rarely saw the lay nuns, apart from Sister Boniface bustling to open the front door with her wide smile. We saw them going up to communion daily in chapel: first the teaching nuns, then the lay sisters, then the girls.

There were lay teachers also, who lived in Paston House in small bed-sitters. Probably unfairly, they seemed to me like caricatures of the spinster teacher of the time. There was Miss Brennan, handsome, dark, who swept along the corridors, her academic gown billowing around her. I felt I could never do anything right for Miss Brennan and our exchanges ('I didn't think, Miss Brennan!' 'You never do think, Paula!') ring down the years. Unfortunately she took us for three of the four subjects we took for Higher Certificate: Latin, History and English (apart from Eng. Lit. taken by Sister Cecilia). Miss Brennan knew her subjects but taught them in the old-fashioned way. I can still see my history notebook: black, smudged writing, page of dates and wars and treaties, reform bills and factory acts. Lessons consisted of taking down these endless notes and learning them by heart for homework. She softened when she taught us about Bonnie Prince Charlie. For her it was a romantic story and we would settle down at our desks, ready for an easy ride while she dreamily wandered up and down talking about him. Like many thinking and intelligent people of the day, she admired Hitler and Mussolini and the improvements they had made for their countries. In our Fifth Form year (1937) she proposed to give a series of lectures on Germany and Italy. Mother Peter cancelled them. The nuns had a very shrewd idea of what was really happening in the Fascist countries as their sister houses there had already met with some persecution.

There was Miss McCormack, who taught us French with the most appalling Irish accent. But she taught well and her lessons were enjoyable, particularly when we had reached the stage of studying French literature: Racine, Mme de Sevigné, Pierre Loti and, for some reason, a treatise by Leon Blum, a Socialist politician, about the reform of the French constitution.

There was gentle Miss Tree, with her round pink cheeks and bright blue eyes, who taught us the sciences. So short-sighted was she that I made sure I sat at the back of the class where, unobserved, I wrote letters and compiled an Arabic-English dictionary. In spite of this, I managed to scrape through one science subject for School Certificate: Botany.

(For School Certificate – GSCE equivalent – we had to take five subjects, of which four had to be English, Maths, a Science and a Modern Language. The fifth subject we all took was Religious Knowledge and as we had learnt the synoptic Gospels by heart, we sailed through that. We worked hard, because if we failed one of the subjects we failed the whole exam and there were no re-takes in those days.)

There was only one non-Catholic lay teacher, Miss Hardy, and it seemed appropriate that she should teach Games and Gym. She was uncomplicated and open and popular. A stocky woman with blonde hair cut in an Eton crop, we never saw her out of her gym slip and it was hard to imagine her private life. (Well, but we didn't expect these women to have any lives apart from teaching us!)

At the Convent in particular we prided ourselves on not being the typical public schoolgirls of the time. "Pashes" were unknown, but for some reason a few of us formed the GPC. The Grand Pash Club would weekly write the names of girls and staff and put them into a bag. Each member would then draw out a name and for the next week have a "pash" on that person. History doesn't relate what the teachers and nuns made of having some girl mooning around them for a week and then losing interest.

Once or twice I had to spend a few weeks at the Convent instead of at Paston. This was when I was in quarantine. Childhood diseases were taken extremely seriously and if one was so much as in contact with an ill child one had to go into quarantine.

One of the advantages of being secluded at the Convent in this way was that one might come in for one of Sister Cecilia's schemes. One term she taught us all the patter songs and the lovelier arias from Gilbert and Sullivan. Another term she set us a competition. We were given a list of classic novels to read and at the end of term there would be a competition to see who knew the novels best. We didn't have the wit to see that this was an educational project and that the "competition" was no more nor less than a test and the conversation at table that term revolved around Mr. Darcy and Becky Sharp and Jane Eyre.

Once I had to have Christmas at the Convent because I was in quarantine for chickenpox and so couldn't go to Mollie Leggitt and her two children as planned. The nuns had arranged that I should go to the Service of Nine Lessons at Kings College Chapel and to Midnight Mass, but in the event I felt unwell and didn't go to either, so it was a subdued Christmas for me. But I was touched on Christmas morning to go into the Study and find about thirty presents wrapped and waiting for me – one present from each sister in the community. I can't remember what they were except for getting a Brownie Box camera, a great prize, which I used for many years. They only cost five shillings (25p) and were of the simplest design but got excellent results.

Holidays – The Leggitts and Others

The end of my first term at Cambridge approached and it seemed that no arrangements had been made for my Christmas holidays – or if they had, they had fallen through. The nuns began to wonder if I should go to their convent in Ascot, where some other girls would go whose parents were abroad.

The problem was solved one day, suddenly it seemed to me, when Mollie Leggitt burst through the front door, wearing a green tweed suit, matching hat perched jauntily on her copper curls and with a red setter on a leash. She swept me up into her car and we drove off to Hitchin where she now lived. The Christmas lights were cheerfully lit in Hitchin and from the moment Mollie tucked me into bed that night, she became a very important person in my life. From then onwards, I was to spend most Christmas and Easter holidays with the Leggitts.

The Leggitts now lived on Hitchin Hill in a small house typical of the ribbon development of the thirties: downstairs there was a kitchen, front room and back room (in which everything happened including the birth of kittens), and upstairs two bedrooms, box room and bathroom. I shared a bedroom with Jeannine (six) and Romalita (four) and Joan, the maid, slept in the box room. Every middle class family, of however limited means, had a live-in maid. Joan was a lumpy, stolid girl with glasses who had come to Mollie from the Waifs and Strays (now the Church of England Children's Society). Her duties were not arduous as Mollie did the shopping and cooking, so much of her time was spent keeping an eye on us. John commuted to London daily.

I found life on Hitchin Hill quite boring. I played "shops" and other simple games with the girls, Mollie took us shopping, we listened to Children's Hour on the radio, followed by Henry Hall and the BBC Dance Band. But I had a bicycle and used to ride into the country or into the town. I was sent "to play with" Sheila Bowen who lived in a large house on Hitchin Hill and we instantly struck up a friendship. Our favourite occupation was to cycle out into the country, playing the "first right, first left" game, having a picnic lunch, then coming home via the signposts. There were few cars and we would dare each other to free-wheel downhill, hands off handlebars, and then collapse in hysterical laughter into the grass verge of the road. Sheila's father owned a flour mill and she had a younger brother, James. More than once recently on a motorway I have spotted a container with the words on the side: James Bowen and Sons, Flour Millers, Hitchin, and it is good to know the family business still flourishes.

Mollie would take us up to London for the day every holidays and the old Roman road, the A1, became extremely familiar. Mollie had been given, by John, a custom-built, scarlet Ford car, a low-slung tourer, and we would speed up to London with the hood down. A familiar experience was to have bus drivers leaning out of their cabs teasing Mollie as she negotiated Trafalgar Square. We must have been an unusual sight as Mollie had striking colouring and looks and the car was stylish but filled with children. And occasionally we would be accompanied by Judy, the red setter.

John Leggitt had turned to public relations as well as journalism and represented (I think) the Spanish Embassy. We often met for a drink, after a day shopping or at a pantomime, at the Spanish Club. Sometimes it was at the Hamilton Club, a small drinking club off Trafalgar Square where media folk met. At Christmas we went to the children's party at the Spanish Embassy (or maybe it was the Spanish Club) – another large, unenjoyable party!

A couple of years after my first Christmas with the Leggitts, they moved to Harpenden, again in Hertfordshire. This time they bought a large house up an unmade road and opposite fields and farms. It was mock Tudor with a large garden which boasted rose and vegetable gardens and a tennis court, as well as a fairly large lawn. Harpenden, at that time, was a commuter town for London and was also a favourite retirement town for ex-Service officers. I often met familiar faces from the Gezira Sporting Club.

At first they were happy times in Harpenden. We had two dogs and two cats, a large garden, the country on our doorstep and the town at the bottom of the hill. We went more frequently to the pictures: first the Shirley Temple and Deanna Durbin films, then the Astaire-Rogers films which I was prepared to see more than once. One could buy a ticket for the first house and sit on through the B film and advertisements and watch the big picture for a second time. A friend and I often did this.

The trips to London continued and a new feature of these was that I now met my mother once every holiday, when we would spend the day together. Her commission was to buy my clothes and she had good taste. As well as shopping, we talked and talked, getting to know one another again.

Sometimes I spent a few days with cousin Lena and her husband Ian in Hendon. Lena told me that on one holiday when I was staying with them, my mother abducted me. I had gone up to the West End to meet her, she had not put me on the train home and nobody knew where she lived. My father and Ian hunted in all the likely places and eventually discovered that she was living with Ardishir in a flat above a shop in the Edgware Road. My only memory of this excitement is of gazing in great boredom out of the sitting-room window at the traffic. Opposite a cinema was showing Richard Tauber in *Springtime in Vienna* and I wished that we could go to see it. The flat itself was small and cramped. Granny Seddall was also living with my mother and Ardishir. I didn't meet the latter and was totally unaware of the drama. As was my wont, I accepted anything that happened to me.

Soon after we moved to Harpenden the atmosphere at home changed radically. In the early days at Hitchin, Mollie and John were openly very much in love. They had met when Mollie was an eighteen-year-old student nurse and had married within four days. This passionate love was apparently still strong. John was usually home early in the evenings and they had put aside Sundays for each other. They would go out for the day for long bicycle rides, leaving us children behind with Joan. By the time we moved to Harpenden, John was working much longer hours and his Sunday mornings were spent largely in bed, surrounded by newspapers from which he gleaned items of interest to Egyptian readers. (Afterwards the papers found their way to the drawing-room, where we pored over them. In those days the reporting of scandals were confined to the *News of the World, Reynolds News* and the *Sunday Mirror* – and then usually in the form of court reports. I used to puzzle over the scoutmasters and curates that often featured in these pages. What *had* they been up to?)

In the course of time something happened to change this apparently idyllic marriage of the Leggitts. Maybe it was a combination of Mollie's personality and John's long working hours, but it soon became obvious that she had embarked on a series of love affairs. She was usually "in love" and would sit dreamily in front of the sitting-room fire when in the throes of another *amour*. But she was quite indiscriminate in her choice of men and quite blatant in her behaviour.

I was extremely distressed at the time. Apart from my own family history, I was now a good Convent girl, with clear ideas of Right and Wrong and Mollie's behaviour was Wrong.

But she mattered too much to me for me to judge or condemn. If my father had known one tenth of what was going on he would have removed me immediately, but of course I never spoke about it to anybody.

(Poor Mollie was to meet her Nemesis when her daughters were both killed in the war. She never got over the tragedy and, I believe, saw it as punishment.)

In 1938 Mollie's brother Gerry joined us in Harpenden. He had been in the Regular Army, a corporal in the Royal Engineers. He had completed his term of service and came to live with Mollie while he looked for work. Gerry and Mollie had belonged to a family of six children of an Essex builder and their mother had died when Gerry was two and Mollie only a few years older. While Mollie was the only one to marry or move into the professional classes, she always remained close to her siblings and Gerry was her absolute favourite.

I had met him once before at a family wedding and marked him down as a cheeky chappie, with Mollie's flirtatious blue eyes and a wide grin of his own. Now he was a self-assured young man of twenty-three, great fun to be with, musical and artistic. It was not long before I succumbed to his considerable charms and in spite of the age gap we became close. Until his death in the Forties, we maintained our bonds of friendship and affection.

Holidays were also spent with other families, of course . . .

. . . the Russells, who lived on a large Air Force base near Felixstowe. Squadron Leader Russell was highly eccentric, even a little mad. A brilliant pianist and artist, an intellectual for a regular officer, he also enjoyed jokes in dubious taste which he would relate at meal times. The rest of us, Mrs. Russell, myself and the two small boys would bear this n embarrassed silence. Mrs. Russell, a quiet, gentle, long-suffering woman, taught me to make toffee and to embroider. For years my poor father had by his bedside a table mat embroidered with the inevitable crinolined lady. I escaped from the house when I needed to, as usual on a bicycle. (During the war, flipping through a *Tatler* at the Turf Club, I found a page of cartoons of an air force base "somewhere in England". There was Arthur Russell, sitting at a typewriter, eyes bulging in anxiety behind his glasses, droplets of sweat leaping from his brow and, tied to the top of his head, a block of ice. Mad as ever!)

. . . the Randalls, who were quite, quite different from the Russells. Stella, Cecily and Clare Randall were all boarders in Cambridge and I was several times invited to stay with them in Limpsfield. Mr. Randall was a diplomat and at that time a delegate to the League of Nations. After the war he was to become our Ambassador in Denmark and although I was invited to join the family there I could never afford to go. Mrs. Randall, a qualified doctor but full-time wife and mother as was customary, had met him when they were students and they had both converted to Roman Catholicism. She was extremely kind to me. Here I was introduced to a rarefied intellectual atmosphere that I had not encountered before. Conversation was lively and I was impressed that Stella was encouraged to sing Schubert lieder in the evenings. The children were not allowed to go to the cinema (they were pitied at school) although this restriction was lifted one holiday when I was there and the youngest child, Martin, and I went to see *The Citadel*. About the corruption of an idealist young doctor who went into private practice, it caused a sensation at that pre-NHS time.

. . . Bee Travis, who was to be my best friend in my last years at Cambridge. She was the only child of a Polish mother and an American father and lived in the beautiful village of

Bibury in the Cotswolds. Bee was a witty, intelligent girl with a zany sense of humour and we would have wonderful days walking and talking in the glorious countryside.

. . . the Fischers. My father's partner, Max Fischer, and his wife had a chateau at Celettes near Blois in the Loire valley and I went to stay with them to brush up my French before Higher School Certificate. My father had been offered a free flight on the new Croydon to Paris service and, telling me he felt nervous of flying himself, he offered it to me! We flew in a small biplane with probably no more than a dozen passengers. We sat, as in a train, in couples facing each other across a table. It was a perfect day, we flew low, and the ships in the channel, the fields of England and France were clearly visible. I was met by a colleague of my father's on the *Continental Daily Mail* who took me out to lunch. He plied me with wine and, at the age of fifteen, I was totally unprepared for its effects. Afterwards I floated down the Champs Elysées, clutching his arm, alarmed at this sudden loss of self-control. I was to get drunk again on this holiday when the Fischers held a wedding anniversary party and Uncle Max offered me a glass of wine with each course. (It was suggested afterwards that I have a siesta with a couple of aspirins.) Ever since I have been wary of drinking too much alcohol! Am not sure I used my French much, apart from talking to the Fischers and the dairy maid while she milked the goat for our daily supply of cheese. Mme. Fischer did take me round the chateaux of the Loire. Otherwise it was a dreamy holiday in such beautiful surroundings.

. . . the Llewellyns.

But, as I have said before, holidays with the Llewellyns were BEST and deserve a chapter to themselves.

The aunts Rosie and Vi with the latter's son John.

Uncle Don Llewellyn.

My father.

On the Convent lawn:
Left: Cecily Randall, self, June Kearans (Sister
Thomas)
Right: Ros McGregor, Stella Randall, June, self,
Clare Randall, Bee Travis (Sister James).

Open Day (for the British). Cairo Airport. 1934.

Cousin Peggy *(centre)* with friends.
Petrified forest, Western Desert. 1936.

The Llewellyns

Holidays with the Llewellyns were the best because I was again with my own family, with its own language, with cousins who were my own age. The atmosphere seemed to me always highly charged. Peggy's energetic enthusiasm, encouraged by Uncle Don, dominated the endless discussions and arguments – about religion, politics, films, fashion, whether we should or should not go to the pictures that night – arguments about everything and anything. Like me, Donald was quieter and gentler, until he reached his teens, when imbued with the public school ethos and gaining self-confidence, he began to fight back on equal terms. Aunt Rosie maintained her usual placid self, quietly keeping the household going, although she was known suddenly to emerge with opinions of such force and wisdom that we would be silenced. Used to moving from one family life style to another, I would remain quiet, chameleon-like, fitting into the background, observing and making note. Nevertheless it was with the Llewellyns that I felt most at ease and at home.

Alternate summers were spent in England when the family would rent a house in Dorset, usually within easy reach of Sandbanks where we had a beach hut. Every possible day was spent on the beach, sunbathing, swimming, making sandcastles and playing games in and out of the gorse bushes.

One summer Uncle Don rented a Dutch yacht barge on the river near Wareham. We also had a dinghy and a motorboat and we would chug off in the latter to Poole Harbour, where we would dive off the side, sometimes swimming to the shore. Uncle Don would swim alongside us, keeping an eye on our ability to swim that far. We befriended two brothers, John and Richard, who were caravanning with their parents nearby. I think the latter considered us rather wild company for their sons, particularly as John and Peggy were conducting a romance. We were rather noisy, I realise. The usual arguments went on endlessly and we had only two records which we played loudly all the time : *Peanuts* and *Rhapsody in Blue*. We would walk along the towpath to the cinema in Wareham, eating fish and chips out of newspaper on the way home. It was at Wareham that for the first time I was emotionally struck by the beauty of the countryside. Coming up on deck one morning, my breath was taken away by the scene on the skyline.

(I believe John was to be killed in the war. I met Richard some years later, still dashingly handsome, a young house officer at the Middlesex Hospital.)

When we were in Dorset we always paid visits to the Llewellyn family in Poole. "Mayflower" was in Longfleet Road, a tall terraced Edwardian house, full of surprise passages and steps. It was lit by gaslight and was always a little spooky. In the front room, Granny Llewellyn reigned: a small white-haired woman, her face disfigured by a lupus of the nose. Stone deaf, she had bright black eyes, which darted around, missing nothing.

I have said elsewhere that the Llewellyns were an old Dorset family, which must sound like a contradiction in terms with such a surname. In 1799 a William Llewellyn, a sea captain, sailed from Wales to Dorset where he remained and founded the dynasty. Granny Llewellyn had added nine children to the clan, of whom Uncle Don was the youngest. Granny Llewellyn was now cared for by the statutory spinster daughter whose life had been devoted to her parents. This was Aunt Gwen, a great favourite with us children. She was a teacher, unfailingly cheerful and a great storyteller. She taught us card games which we were to play well into adulthood. The only other uncle I remember was Uncle Edgar, the eldest of the brood who had an impressive moustache and Communist sympathies. He was intent on educating us and would take us round the London museums, which I found so boring that I was put off going inside a museum for a long time. I have a memory of him fiddling with the crystal radio set in an effort to get the National Programme, the precursor of Radio 4. I also remember Granny Llewellyn gathering us round while she read the sorry tale of Tennyson's *Lucy Gray*.

Sometimes we would be joined at Mayflower by another Llewellyn cousin, Marian. She was older than us, a sweet gentle dark girl, whose long hair was styled in the fashion of the time: parted in the middle and coiled in "telephones" round each ear. Marion was to become a paintress at Poole Pottery and I always look for her "sign", a cross, on the pottery of the period. Later she was to marry Dr. David Greenham, a horticulturist at East Malling Research Station, and she was to remain one of our favourite cousins until her death in the Nineties.

The most extraordinary and memorable holidays of the time were the summer holidays spent in Egypt. Every alternate summer my cousins went out to Cairo to join their parents and on two occasions, in 1934 and 1936, when I was eleven and thirteen respectively, I went with them.

In those days there were many, many British families in the Mediterranean whose children were at boarding school in England and the P&O ran "children's boats" to cope with them – two going out at the beginning of the summer holidays, two returning at the end. There would be about two hundred children on board of all ages, travelling in Tourist Class. The First Class accommodated adults and a few bewildered adults joined us in Tourist. In charge of our welfare, apart from the busy ship's officers, were two matrons, whose prime occupation we soon realised was to flirt with the ship's officers. The only times I remember a matron getting involved with us was once to ask us to put cotton wool in our ears when we swam (we paid no attention) and presumably when one of the boys went down with mumps.

In spite of this, no harm came to us, much. Alcohol was unobtainable, the word "drugs", if ever used, would have referred to medicines and although sex could hardly be ignored among so many adolescents, I was aware of few breaches of our moral code. For we had a deeply inculcated sense of what was and was not "done". The two seventeen-year-olds who conducted an open love affair were envied (she was blonde and beautiful) but not approved. There were a few other transgressions of the code (day-time "bundling" in one of the cabins, kissing games on top deck after dinner), but they were only by a handful of children.

For many of us, like me, were protected by our innocence. At the age of thirteen I did not know the "facts of life" and when they were to be crudely described to me the following year by my friend Bee it sounded so ridiculous that I bet her five shillings (five weeks' pocket money) she was wrong. (I owe you, Bee!). On the voyage out when I was thirteen I acquired a boyfriend: Dennis Naldrett Jays, the son of the Chief of Police in Alexandria. Our love-making consisted of lying side by side sun-bathing and talking by the pool and gazing shyly into one another's eyes – strictly no touching.

On the last night of the voyage Pamela Jarman, a boy called Felix, Dennis and I decided we would sleep on deck. We found a lifeboat and settled down for the night, side by side, innocently but romantically beneath a full moon and the Mediterranean sky, studded with brilliant stars. Before long a bright torch shone into the boat and the shocked voice of a ship's officer told us to get out. 'We want to sleep on deck!' we protested. He yielded by producing four deck chairs in which we slept and woke, shivering, to the sailors swabbing down the decks at dawn. During the holidays Dennis wrote to me regularly from Alexandria, but on the return journey to England another lively brunette attracted him away from me.

The sailing from England at the beginning of the holidays was an event in itself. Accompanied on the train to Tilbury Docks by my mother and Granny Seddall, we would all go aboard, go down below to inspect our cabins, renew old friendships. Then the ship's siren would go and my mother and grandmother went ashore to wave us goodbye as we sailed off, pilot's tug chuffing importantly beside us.

The first days of the journey out were quiet, exploratory, while we got to know the cabin mate allotted to us, learnt the lay of the ship and formed cliques of friends.

Then we hit the Bay of Biscay. Liners had not been equipped with the stabilisers they have today, and the ship would toss and shudder in the notorious bay's weather. Most people were seasick. Donald and I were good sailors and were among only about a dozen people who would make their way up on deck to avoid the sickness that would attack if we stayed below. We would cling to the rails, buffeted by fierce winds, soaked by the spray.

Soon we would be in calmer waters and would sail into Gibraltar, where we anchored for a day. We always went ashore, wandering up Main Street, buying a few souvenirs. In 1936, at the height of the Spanish Civil War, whether by accident or design I don't remember, Donald and I wandered into No Man's Land as far as the Spanish frontier, when we were sent packing by angry soldiers.

The ship would move on to Tangier, but would anchor well offshore so that we couldn't leave the ship. Soon we would be surrounded by small boats selling us souvenirs. We would pull them up by rope in a basket, choose our goods, haggle at top voice and sent the money back down.

After Tangier, we stopped at Marseilles, sometimes for as much as two days for re-coaling. We were strictly forbidden to go ashore unaccompanied by an adult, but we got round this. Felix, who was an inveterate mischief-maker, would cause a disturbance. The sailor guarding the gangplank would go to deal with it and a few of us scuttled ashore. It was incredibly boring on the docks in Marseilles! We could not see what the fuss was about. After desultorily wandering around the bales and other impedimenta that cluttered the ground, we went aboard again.

Finally, Malta, beautiful in its gleaming white simplicity against the blue sea. Adding to the spectacle in 1936 were the British warships which filled Valetta harbour. The Spanish Civil War was seen as a serious threat to world peace and has since been seen as the forerunner of the Second World War.

By now the sun was shining merrily and the canvas swimming pool had been erected on deck and filled with seawater. What we called a "good Captain" would take a pro-active interest in us and arrange several entertainments for us: Bingo, a treasure hunt, a fancy dress dance, etc.

One captain arranged for a party to go down to the engine room. It was a glimpse of Hell: the railings were hot to the touch and below us we could see the Sikh stokers, hair tucked up, naked to the waist, bodies gleaming with sweat, shovelling the coal into the huge blazing furnaces.

We danced every evening. There were two sittings for meals, the early one for the under-twelves, the second for the older children. When I was only eleven, I slipped into the late session unchallenged and with the others changed like an adult for dinner, with a view to dancing afterwards. The boys put on their suits, we put on our party dresses. I still remember the thrill of hearing, as I left my cabin, the sound down the airshafts of the band playing *Let's Face the Music and Dance.* Donald, like his father, was a beautiful ballroom dancer and all evening we would whirl round the dance floor together – until the band played *Whispering* and we knew the evening was over.

When we arrived at Port Said Uncle Don would be waiting for us with his open tourer and we would drive through the Nile Delta, on a dusty unmade road through the fields of *berseem* and cotton, in which we could see the *fellahin* (peasants) bending over the crops, their *galabiehs* tucked up and tied round their waists revealing their legs. As we went through each village the women, gracefully carrying their earthenware water pots on their heads would stop to stare. The Arab children, the boys in their *galabiehs,* the girls in bright coloured dresses, would run out to wave and shout their welcome: *"Sayeeda! Sayeeda!"* We would wave and shout back *"Sayeeda! Sayeeda!"*

We were home!

My father would be coming out to Egypt, but he arrived later than we did. The first summer holiday I went to the Llewellyns until I could join him in his pretty flat nearby, overlooking the Casino. The second trip out, I went straight to his flat, which he had lent to Roseen Preston, whose mother had been Mollie Graves with whom my father had fallen in love many years before. Mollie Graves was now married to Judge Preston, a judge in the Egyptian High Court and I am not at all sure why Roseen had borrowed our flat. Roseen was glamorous. In her twenties, fair and elegant, she went riding at Mena early in the morning and came home to breakfast, often with a handsome swain in tow. Most impressive of all, she had an Italian lady's maid who brought me tea and biscuits in bed in the morning.

The daytimes were, of course, spent with my cousins. And as had been customary, they were usually spent at the swimming pool.

But what a transformation had taken place while we had been away at school!

The swimming pool had before been surrounded by non-descript buildings housing the changing rooms. These had been swept away to be replaced by spacious luxurious changing rooms, with a rest room and hairdressers on the women's side. Near the men's changing rooms there were new kitchens and above them sunbathing terraces. Between these rooms and the pool there was now a terrace with small tables and chairs for refreshments. The pool was open to the polo field and was supplemented by a children's pool and a paddling pool. A fountain divided the main pool from the smaller ones. The architecture was beautiful and it now was to become a pleasure to sit there both summer and winter. It was christened The Lido and became a popular gathering place, particularly for the young, where we would swim, sunbathe, gossip and flirt. Sometimes we spent the day there having for lunch one of the delicious sandwiches and a *limoun moya* (fresh lime and water) or a Campbell's: our favourite drink of fizzy lemonade, angostura bitters, lemon and ice. Just as we had behaved like young adults on board ship, so we now lounged in the basket chairs, clapping our hands to be served by the waiters in their spotless white *galabiehs*, scarlet wide sashes and *tarbooshes*.

Before the holidays began a committee of parents was formed at the club to devise entertainments for us and no doubt each father tried to out-do the others . . .

. . . Uncle Don organised a weekend camp in the desert, near to the Shell Resthouse where we could get meals. We were also near a petrified forest and to the Wadi Natrun Monastery, one of the oldest monasteries in existence, both of which we visited. The monastery, which had been founded in the third century was still extremely primitive, the conditions simple and harsh. Since then the monks have cultivated the surrounding desert and have become famous for their vineyards and horticultural methods. The community has grown spectacularly, mainly with professional Copts, but the regime of austerity, work and prayer remain the same.

. . . Mr. Cross, General Manager of Imperial Airways (the forerunner of BA and the only airway to control the airport), organised a day trip to Cairo Airport where we were able to inspect the planes and to have trips over the city. We were impressed to find the plane could go at 80 mph. (Were there *no* commercial flights that day?)

. . . There was a swimming gala in which anyone could take part.

. . . There was a Fathers v Sons cricket match and one between the boys of the Gezira and the Ma'adi Sporting Clubs.

. . . There was a trip by Nile steamer up the river to the Barrage in the Delta, which boasted beautiful botanical gardens and where we picnicked and watched the *gulli-gulli* man. He was a conjuror who could produce live chicks from behind your ear or yards of coloured streamers from his mouth. These men never failed to fascinate. On the journey home, Uncle Don inevitably organised a sing-song round the piano.

. . . There was a sports day at the club racecourse and, as well as the usual egg and spoon and sack races, etc., there was a donkey race. I have a photograph of Peggy helplessly laughing as she tried to urge her donkey into moving.

. . . There was the Children's Dance at the Club, usually towards the end of the summer. On one occasion when the band broke for refreshment, we took over. Some boys got on to the piano and timpani and the rest of us found what we could to play. I brandished the caracas. We must have made a hideous noise and I have not forgotten the looks of horror on the musicians' faces when they returned.

Then there were the private parties, usually dances in people's homes, although one family gave a desert party near the Pyramids.

We went to the open-air cinemas, in one of which, the St. James or "Jimmy's", one was distracted by the sounds emanating from the open-air cinema next door. Jimmy's was also a popular restaurant and in later years I learnt that the clever trick was to book the one particular table over-looking the cinema next door and from which one could watch two films at once!

Uncle Don thought it should be part of our education to go to nightclubs and took us out to cabarets, particularly the Kit Kat across the river, where we could dance and watch reputedly the best belly dancer in Egypt.

The days went hectically and swiftly past and soon it would be time to return to England and school.

We grew up fast in those Cairo holidays. Having been trusted to behave responsibly on board ship, on the whole we did behave sensibly, in spite of the fun and high spirits. The social and sexual mores of the time protected us, so that we flirted and imagined we fell in love, but little harm came to us.

Peggy, already fourteen on our first trip out, grew up the fastest. By the time she was sixteen she was wearing high heels and had had her striking blonde hair permed. With her beautiful blue eyes and husky come-hither voice, she usually had a boyfriend in tow. Her opinions on everything became more vehement – the arts, books, politics, men – all were pronounced upon with ever greater conviction. Certainly she has been proved right in her views on the arts, particularly the cinema. Her views on politics and men I absorbed thoughtfully.

Donald developed over those years from an amusing mischievous boy into another vociferous member of the family, usually arguing in opposition to his sister. He and I had our separate friends and interests, but we were very close. While Peggy was a striking blonde, Donald and I were both slender and dark and were often mistaken for brother and sister. Peggy was my leader and mentor and I admired her inordinately, but I was so completely at ease with Donald that he might have been my twin, I felt.

As for Jane, I have little memory of her during those holidays, apart from the fact that we learnt that she could swim at the age of four and I have photographs to prove it. She must have led her own personal life (aged then about four and six) in the nursery and playground with her nanny.

I saw very little of my father. He arrived in Egypt a week or so after we did. He and I met at breakfast and sometimes he would put in an appearance at a party or other social function, but we were content, he and I, that I should spend most of the time with the cousins.

I can have no objective view of what those holidays meant to me. I can only say that my instant memory is of unalloyed pleasure, although there must have been some bad times. I do remember that as a result of sunbathing too long at the Lido I had had to spend a few days in bed, lying on my stomach, waiting for the fever to drop while Aunt Rosie dabbed my shoulders with calamine lotion. Then there was the unpleasant occasion when an elderly sailor on board ship attempted to molest me. So, after all, we must have been at some risk, although we never felt this and our parents seemed free of anxieties on our behalf.

I learned nothing new about Egypt. Our privileged world was still enclosed by the island and the Club and we were children of our time. Sure, there was poverty and injustice in Egypt, but so there was in England. There we had seen the long, long dole queues, the depressed tramps moving from town to town, children playing, shoeless, in the streets – this was the way of the world it seemed to us. Uncle Don and Peggy must have expressed their Socialist views, but at the time I personally was untouched by them. Perhaps I was too busy growing up and that was enough to contend with.

The antiquities of Egypt we took for granted, much as an English child would wander through Trafalgar Square, uninterested in Nelson's Column, but fascinated by the buses and pigeons. The Pyramids served as a backdrop to Mena House Hotel and desert picnics. The Sphinx was notable because the only way to see it was to hire a camel or donkey and ride across the desert sands. I didn't visit the pyramids at Sakkara until I went with friends to show them to some Army officers during the war. Upper Egypt and its wonders were an unknown quantity. There was more talk among adults of the duck shooting in the Siwa Oasis than of Luxor and Aswan.

During those Egyptian holidays I renewed my friendship with Joan Hooper with whom I had got up to mischief when we were nine. She is now a great-grandmother living near Toronto and in a recent Christmas card she referred to "those happy Cairo days."

Yes, indeed!

Gathering Clouds

The last two or three years at the Convent were memorably the happiest of my time there. The nuns believed in stretching their pupils and I was to take Senior School Certificate (GCSE equivalent) at the age of fourteen and Higher (A Level equivalent) two years later. Academic work was a strain therefore, but it went with the pleasures and privileges of the Fifth and Sixth Forms. And in any case we were still children and we knew how to enjoy ourselves.

Memories of the work fade beside such memories as weekends lazing in the garden playing the gramophone – *Night and Day, I've got you under my skin, Stardust.* That was the era of Cole Porter and Jerome Kern and Gershwin and we knew their music by heart. Winter evenings in the Study reading, arguing, pursuing our hobbies of stamp collecting, etc; listening to Radio Luxembourg; playing tennis after supper in the summer; riding round the garden on our bikes (a great craze, the riding of bicycles).

One autumn term we returned to find a new wing had been built on to the Convent. On the top floor were five single rooms for girls whose parents were prepared to pay extra, new nuns' cells on the first floor and new extended kitchens on the ground floor. My father was prepared to pay the extra cost and I moved into the new wing. We five girls considered ourselves very special and christened ourselves the Dionne Quins, after the first quins to survive who had recently been born in Canada. We were Stella and Cecily Randall, Hilary Clay, who was a weekly boarder and lived in Cambridge, and Rosamund McGregor, the daughter of Indian Army parents, who spent holidays with grandparents in Camberley, and myself. We further christened our floor the Champs Elysées, and the bathroom the Queen Mary after the new trans-Atlantic liner.

I loved my private room with its pretty curtains and furnishings. I had a washbasin in the corner and a desk at the end of the bed. In the Sixth Form years I was allowed to study in my room and have my light out an hour after anyone else.

Another pleasure in these years was that, although I didn't excel in sport, I was in the Convent tennis and netball teams because our numbers were so low that all the older girls were enlisted. It meant that we, in the team, had extra tennis coaching from Mr. Deer, a Davis Cup player, and tennis became more enjoyable.

In spite of our comparatively cloistered life we were increasingly aware of events in the political world. A copy of the *Daily Telegraph* had always awaited us each evening in the Study. We had all been affected, either personally or through friends and family, by the Depression. During those dark days I could see, every morning from my bedroom window, about two dozen tramps sitting outside the kitchens drinking mugs of hot tea and chunks of bread and butter brought to them by the nuns. Tramps were rightly so called because they could not stay more than one night at a time in men's hostels, so each day they moved to the next town and they knew that there the local convent would provide food and drink.

On the occasion of the Abdication in 1936 we had all been summoned to sit in a solemn circle in the School and listen to Edward VIII's abdication speech. We had long hated Mrs. Simpson and our autograph books were full of rude verses about her. By the end of the speech many of us, including me, were in tears.

Bee's uncle had been a war correspondent in Abyssinia when Mussolini invaded and he sent her vivid accounts of the war, which she shared with us. We followed the Spanish Civil

War with interest – one new girl was a refugee from Barcelona.

And in spite of the Munich Agreement in 1938, a pact between Germany and England that Hitler would make no further advances in Europe, there grew the sickening certainty that we were heading for war.

In my 1939 diary, among the schoolgirl silliness and exclamation marks, there are entries in capital letters such as:

. . . (March 1939) HITLER ENTERS BOHEMIA AND TAKES PRAGUE.

. . . (March 1939) HITLER HAS MADE TERMS WITH HUNGARY.

. . . (April 1939) MUSSOLINI TOOK ALBANIA.

. . . (June 1939) JAPANESE BLOCKADE ENGLISH. GERMANY SUPPORTS JAPAN.

. . . (July 1939) OUTBREAK OF IRA BOMB OUTRAGES. (For the Irish Question has always been with us.)

Then, in the summer term of 1939 we were distributed with gas masks. Hideous frightening things which fortunately were never needed in the war to come.

There were two important publishing events in the late thirties which were to revolutionise our thinking. The first was the founding of the Penguin paperbacks. There had only been hardback books published in England until then. The French had favoured paperbacks, but they were poorly bound. Penguin Books were of good quality and, most importantly, only sixpence each, well within the bounds of our pocket money. One of the first Penguins was called *I was Hitler's Prisoner* by Stefan Zweig, which opened our eyes to the Nazi regime. Although we knew the Jews and Catholics were subject to persecution, we had not understood the full extent of this. We were only to learn about the concentration camps towards the end of the war.

Stefan Zweig, a Hungarian Jewish refugee and journalist, then edited *Picture Post,* the first magazine printed by rotogravure in this country and the first mainly pictorial magazine. For the first time social issues were dealt with boldly and "ordinary people" appeared in its pages. To our fascinated delight in one of the first issues there was a feature on Cambridge University and some of the undergraduates lodging with Mary Howitt were photographed.

The combination of the Penguin books and Picture Post was revolutionary. We read both avidly and began to understand more about our society than we ever had before.

More clouds were forming in my personal life.

To my surprise, when I was confirmed at the age of twelve my white Confirmation dress was made by the same boring friend of my father's, Miss Ingle, as had made my First Communion dress. Moreover, she came to the service in the parish church and took me out to lunch afterwards. She was still boring. A great many of my father's women friends had taken an interest in me and they had all been either kind and motherly, like Mrs. Vernon Jarvis, or sharp-witted and amusing like Aunty Carty and Mme. Fischer. Miss Ingle was neither: a reserved woman with whom I seemed to have nothing in common.

She then appeared by my father's side the following summer holidays and we would drive off for trips in a car my father had hired. (The brakes didn't work and whenever my father stopped on a hill, Miss Ingle and I would leap out and stick a brick under the rear wheels!) On one such trip we went to visit her brother's family near Chichester and having drinks in the yacht club I heard Miss Ingle address my father as "darling". I decided I had misheard.

But in 1938 I received a letter from my father telling me he intended to marry Miss Ingle. I was horrified and wrote back passionately to persuade him that he should not do this. He could not do it. He was a Catholic and he would be committing a mortal sin in marrying again while his first wife was still alive. This seemed to me a winning argument. But my father's next letter was to tell me that they had already married. This really was a shock, as I had never even accepted that my parents were divorced. Mollie had been delegated the job of telling me that they were, but when she did so one evening sitting by the fire in Harpenden I had said 'Yes, I know. I know,' thinking to myself, 'These stupid Protestants. Because my parents are separated they think they must automatically be divorced. But they can't be. They're Catholics.'

Well, the deed was done and I would have to accept it. I was enjoined by my father not to tell the nuns, but of course they must have known. References were often enough to be made to Mr. and Mrs. Philip Taylor in the society pages of *The Sphinx* and Sister Cecilia read that from cover to cover before passing it on to me. She pointed out one such reference to me questioningly, but I declared it must be a mistake and she never referred to it again. Mother Peter raised it once, and then on my last day at school, and then only obliquely.

Secrets, secrets – the many secrets of my childhood! And there was one more to be kept before I left school, but first I must fill in Miss Ingle's background.

Joan Ingle was one of three children of an English bank manager in Bangalore, India, and a French mother. At the age of four she was sent to England to board at the Convent of the Holy Child Jesus near Blackpool. I had occasion in my twenties to visit this school and my heart bled for the small child from India being sent to this forbidding building on a hill surrounded by bleak landscape and fierce winds, however kind the nuns may have been. When she left school she returned to Bangalore and was to tell me of exciting rides on horseback and tiger hunts when she would spend the night up a tree waiting for her prey. After two or three years she was asked to accompany her younger brother Louis to boarding school in England and decided to stay on in London and train as a nurse at Guy's Hospital. She enjoyed the London life of the twenties and the hospital fancy dress balls. Every winter she would go skiing in Switzerland.

Then she went to Egypt and got a job at the Anglo-American Hospital in Cairo. It was there she met and nursed my father through pneumonia. In those days the only cure for this killer disease was highly skilled nursing and one can imagine that a close bond was formed between them both. She then got a job at the Kitchener Memorial Hospital in Cairo, a charity hospital for poor Egyptians and, after some struggles with their consciences (they were both Roman Catholics), my father and Joan got married. But by the time they did marry, she had contracted tuberculosis and had had both sanatorium treatment and a pneumothorax: the surgical collapse of one lung which then had to be inflated with air medically at regular intervals. It was the most up-to-date treatment of the day, but was to lead to problems for her in the war years.

In fairness I must add that she proved to be a good and loving wife to my father, for whom she could never do enough. It took some months, if not years, for Joan Ingle and me to be on easy terms, but we ended good and mutually supportive friends.

The other secret that had to be kept from the nuns was that Mollie Leggitt had met her *coup de foudre* in John Clark, whom she had met at the Hamilton Club. He was divorced and unlike most of the members of the club was not in the media but worked in his family's business of refining sugar for breweries. Mollie had left her husband to live with John and her two daughters in a small village in Kent. My father thoroughly disapproved of this action and once again it was understood that it should be kept secret from the nuns. And once again, they clearly knew what had happened.

And what of my mother of whom I have made little mention in these pages?

I continued to meet her once every Christmas and Easter holidays and more frequently in the summer. We usually spent the day in Oxford Street, eating at the Marble Arch Corner House, shopping for clothes, drinking endless cups of tea and talking. We got on well and I was developing as she would have wished me to do. It was only after the war when she met me again and didn't like what she saw that she would criticise me relentlessly and hurtfully.

She had ambitions for me, some quite unrealistic. One was that I should go to the Royal College of Music and learn the harp. She thought it a beautiful instrument, but it held no interest for me. Another was that I should go to the School of Oriental Languages and enter the consular service or Foreign Office. Finally, she hit on an idea which appealed to me enormously: that I should stay at school a further two years studying my favourite subjects of English, French and Music and when I was eighteen and eligible, go up to Cambridge University. I already knew that in those two years the nuns would give me great freedom to go into town and to attend extra-mural lectures and I longed to go to university. Moreover the nuns hoped I would do so. However, my father turned down the plan, as I suspected he would, saying he couldn't afford it. His dream was that I should join him in Cairo, get a secretarial job at the Embassy and doubtless make a good marriage.

In any case the war intervened and put an end to any dreams.

The last term came and went in a flurry of activity and hectic revising interspersed with tests. On the day before our Higher exams started we went on the annual outing to Laburnum Woods. It was felt it was best to clear our minds before embarking on the exams. We certainly enjoyed ourselves that year: "June, Bee and I got lost in wheat fields! Marvellous fun. Lovely little villages! Made friends with cottager. Got home dead tired."

Suddenly it was the last day and Mother Peter came out to say goodbye to me in the garden. She hoped I would be happy and would make a good marriage and not be affected by neither my parents' fate nor that of Mollie's. I don't remember my reply. All I remember is that I was in tears.

I was leaving behind the security and affection the convent had given me in the previous six years. I had grown in confidence and self-esteem and, although in many ways unprepared for the storms of adult life, I had been offered a moral code and introduced to a spiritual life which were to serve as a bedrock.

And the future looked bleak and uncertain.

The Summer before the Storm

But before facing this future there was the summer to be enjoyed.

To start with I went camping, something I had never done before – at least not jolly schoolgirl camping, the thought of which was anathema to any Cambridge convent girl. The camp was organised by the Grail, then a Catholic girls' youth organisation which paid particular attention to school leavers. We had heard about it during our last term at school and because it sounded different and might be fun two of us decided to give it a try. That flippant schoolgirl decision was to prove momentous.

The camp was held in the grounds of Ashburnham House near Battle, the home of an old Catholic family. We were under canvas and it *was* all very jolly. I hated it at first. We all took turns at different jobs – Drawer of Water, Feeder of the Multitude, etc. We had lectures, went for walks, were entertained, and after supper we had a sing-song round a campfire. Halfway through the ten days I was completely converted to the way of life and to the Grail's ideals, and by the end of the camp had joined up to be a Grail member.

(All through the coming war I was to receive their magazine, which was of an unusually high quality both in presentation and content, and after the war my first London job was to work in Grail Publications in Sloane Street. A fellow Grail member, Marjorie Courtney, gave a party one night at the flat in Nevern Square she shared with her mother. During the evening I noticed a tall blonde god on the dance floor. Eventually he asked me to dance and later he escorted my friend Pat Marmion and me home to our digs in Sloane Gardens.

Eight years later we were to get married.)

After the camp I joined my father and stepmother Joan in their hotel in the Cromwell Road. Shortly after, we set off on a tour of the South coast in our hired car. First stop Hastings, where I saw Lawrence Olivier in a memorable *Wuthering Heights,* then showing in a local cinema. Then on to Deal where we were to stop, as Joan knew an ex-patient who had become a friend. Thelma Stannard lived with her parents in a large house on the cliffs overlooking Deal. Her mother bred St. Bernard dogs.

After two days I was informed that I was to stay behind in Deal while my father and Joan continued their tour. Thelma knew of a family who took in children whose parents were abroad and they agreed to have me. The family was headed by "the Captain", an unpleasant man with a rat-like face and thin black moustache. His wife was quiet, nondescript. There were perhaps four other children of different ages in the house. I only half-understood it then, but am virtually certain now that the Captain was either having an affair, or trying to, with the eldest girl, an unhappy blonde teenager.

Thelma took me out most days. She took me to the pictures or to coffee with friends in the town. One friend told us with wonder that her public school son who had joined up in the ranks was finding that his fellow 'working-class chaps were really quite good fellows.' It has been said before, but if there was one good thing that came out of the war it was that class barriers were broken down and public schoolboys began to understand how the less privileged lived: an understanding that was to give support to the post-war Welfare State from all political parties.

Mostly Thelma and I talked, walking along the front, hearing faint music from the Royal Marines College of Music. She talked a little too freely about her love life and with typical sibling rivalry about her sister who was so obsessed by ballet that she could think and talk of nothing else. She had recently taken the professional name of Ninette de Valois.

And so back to Cromwell Road. There were only three or four weeks before we would have to sail for Egypt.

The atmosphere in London had changed. It was a nervy, edgy time. The Russians and Germans had just made a pact and the threat of a full European war hung over us. The Cromwell Road was strangely empty of much traffic. People walked past one with a subdued look. Public buildings were being sand-bagged as protection from bombs. Notices were appearing to indicate the nearest air-raid shelter. To add to the general air of anxiety, the IRA decided to step up their bombing campaign. Extraordinary to relate, but one day I was at Kings Cross Station and just missed an explosion and only two days later I just missed another at Victoria Station.

For I was moving around a lot in those last weeks, making farewells – to Finchley to cousins Lena and Ian; to Limpsfield to the Randalls, where I found to my delight that Bee was staying; to Gloucester Road to visit another school-friend; to Kew where the Llewellyns now lived in a flat near the Gardens. Donald and Jane were still at school, Donald in his final year. Peggy was a student at the Central School of Art and the flat was swarming with interesting and entertaining young men and women. Granny Seddall was also there, but frail and by now an alcoholic. She was to die within the next year.

Back at Cromwell Road Joan was preparing to travel back to Egypt. My father was feverishly trying to get a passage as his original bookings had been cancelled. Two close friends of my parents were also at the hotel, Mootie and Edgar de Knevett.

Suddenly Joan made a gesture which threw me into shock and misery. It sounds a trivial enough incident but to me it was a blow. The sensational film of the year was *The Four Feathers* and it had been suggested that we should go to see it. I was truly excited. But when I went to get ready to go out, Joan told me that the outing was not for me but it was for the grown-ups, for themselves and the de Knevetts. I was appalled. It would have been inconceivable for Mollie or the Llewellyns or the Randalls not to include the younger members of the family in an excursion to the cinema. For years I had been treated like a young adult and now I was being firmly put in the place Joan believed I belonged – the nursery. I had taken the Dumping at Deal in my stride because I was always being farmed out, but this was an insult. I spent a miserable evening in the cavernous gloomy hotel, brooding and angry.

I mention this contretemps because it was to set back my relationship with Joan by many months. It can't have been easy for the poor woman, recently married and deeply in love with my father and inexperienced in dealing with young people, let alone a sullen teenager. For my part, in spite of the difficulties of my childhood – probably because of them – my father had always indulged me. My slightest wish was his command, if it was within his power to deliver. In fact, I was thoroughly spoilt by him. We had also become very good friends and Joan now intruded on our relationship. For his part, my father had his own concerns. His immediate task was to get us all safely back to Egypt and for the next few months he was to struggle to keep us afloat financially. The last thing he needed was to have to enter into the problems of his womenfolk.

I go into this in some detail because my reaction to my father's remarriage was in part to influence my subsequent behaviour in Cairo and therefore my experience of the war there.

Before Alamein we had no victories:
After Alamein we had no defeats.
Winston Churchill

WARTIME CAIRO
1939-1945

Return to Egypt

We were in Kent the day the war broke out. I was staying with Mollie and John Clark in Wilmington; my parents in a small pub in a nearby village.

September 3, 1939, a Sunday, was a beautiful autumn day, sunny and warm and the blue sky above was cloudless. We had all gathered round the radio to listen to Neville Chamberlain's weary voice as he told us he had delivered an ultimatum to Hitler to stop his invasion of Poland. If he did not do so by eleven o'clock on the Sunday he could consider himself to be at war with England and France. Nothing had been heard from Germany and we realised we were now irrevocably on the verge of another Great War.

My parents and I met that morning to go to Mass in their village. A few minutes after the service had started the air raid sirens wailed. For the first time, I was petrified. We had heard of the all-out bombing of Poland, Hitler had already taken Czechoslovakia, the Saar and Austria and we knew he aimed to conquer Britain. Kent was directly under the flight path to London and I imagined bombs raining down on us at any minute. The priest paused, then turned round and said quietly that he would continue with the Mass.

The siren was famously a false alarm and soon the long sustained note of the all-clear sounded. But it was a bad few moments.

We tried to carry on life as normally as possible although my father made frequent trips to London, either on business or to arrange our passage back to Egypt. Mollie had already put up blackout curtains of a cheap black cotton. Evacuees arrived in the village from London. On the night of September 3 when the pub opposite closed, the men poured out singing *'Run, Rabbit Run'* and *'We're going to hang out our washing on the Siegfried Line'* (Germany's defence system along the border with France). I wondered if this was going to be a war like the last when the troops sang their way into battle, but in the event this was not to be the case. For the next two years or so we were going to contemplate the possibility of defeat and in any case it was a more sophisticated generation going into uniform.

After tearful farewells, my parents and I returned to the Cromwell Hotel.

There were more tears when I said goodbye to my mother at the same banal location that I had met her for the first time after the four years' silence: Marble Arch Underground Station. I was frozen and tearless, but my mother wept copiously. She was grieving two losses. I was leaving for Egypt and there was no guarantee we would meet again. Ardishir was in hospital following a serious car accident and she 'could not visit him. Only his wife was entitled to do that.' He was to die a few weeks later.

I rang Aunt Rosie in Kew to make my farewells.

'Are you looking forward to going back to Cairo?' she asked.

'Yes' I lied. I ached to stay in England to help in the war effort. But she saw through me and a typically dry 'H'm' came down the phone before she warmly and affectionately hoped I would be happy.

We left for Egypt a fortnight after war broke out. We were to travel across France to pick up a boat in Marseilles. Our first taste of the problems ahead was met at Folkestone where we had to go through customs. The de Knevetts were in our party and also our family solicitor, Teddy Hyam. The latter was a Jew, the kindest of men but one of the uglier men I have known with a hooked nose, swarthy complexion and a slight cast in his eyes. The customs official took against him and, while the rest of us were let through the inspection lightly,

Teddy was subjected to utmost humiliation. Every pair of socks was unrolled, family photographs torn from their frames, every corner of his suitcases examined. The customs officer found nothing incriminating, of course, so resorted to stripping Teddy of all his cash. He was being expected to travel across the continent and to Egypt with no money – no credit cards then. He had to become dependant on the rest of us to support him financially, although we were not allowed to take more than £20 each out of the country. Fortunately, Joan had stuffed rolls of bank notes into the tops of her stockings. I have often wondered how she would have fared if she had been searched, but her face was at all times the picture of innocence. Well, at least we had enough money between us for our journey.

As we sailed from Folkestone, escorted by the RAF, I left our party who were discussing the possibility of Indian troops being sent to the Middle East, to lean on a rail and watch England grow smaller. More misery! It felt like desertion to be leaving the country so recently at war and I wanted to help its defence.

The journey to Paris seemed interminable. Having boarded the train at Boulogne, we had to wait nearly five hours before it moved off, blacked-out and packed with French troops. We arrived in Paris at midnight and were to stay there two nights before leaving for Marseilles. I record the delicious meals we ate, usually with my father's colleagues from the *Continental Daily Mail*. But the talk was gloomy, particularly as while we were there Russia also invaded Poland.

We took another packed, blacked-out train to Marseilles, again arriving in the middle of the night. We couldn't board our ship, so my father set out into the dark to find a hotel. After what seemed an age he returned with the news that a small hotel called *Le Petit Palais* had rooms. What a misnomer! It was a sordid little establishment near the docks.

The proprietress led me to my room at the top of the house. It had two doors, one of which adjoined the next bedroom. As she left me for the night the woman repeated twice, pointing to the latter door, *'N'ayez pas peur! N'ayez pas peur!'* When she was gone, I was so frightened that I didn't dare go to the lavatory across the landing. I pushed chairs up against both doors and lay down on my bed fully clothed to the sound of what seemed to be the constant tearing up of paper from the next room. I did fall asleep and the night proved uneventful. The next morning we left after Teddy Hyam had demanded a reduction in the cost because he had all night been bitten by bed bugs.

The ship was overcrowded and my parents and I had to share a cabin with a strange woman. We had to take turns getting up in the morning and going to bed at night – me first. Otherwise it was a comfortable voyage of perhaps five days before we landed in Egypt.

This trip was memorable for me for the friendships I made on board. We were a group of five, Desmond O'Meara, a slim blonde boy, Peggy and Desmond Smouha, all returning from public schools in England, and Nimet Cattaoui, returning from holidays in Switzerland and France. We walked the decks and talked earnestly, as only teenagers can.

The Smouhas and Nimet were Egyptian Jews ('We're pure Egyptian Jews' Desmond was to declare solemnly and proudly one night on top deck). His father was immensely rich and owned a large swathe of Alexandria known as Smouha City and which included the Sporting Club. Speaking like a Crown Prince, he said he would love to be an explorer but 'I suppose I will have to take on the business and marry one of the Ades girls.' (The Ades family was another large Jewish clan based in Cairo. I knew the girls well and in the event they all married English officers during the war.)

The most interesting fact to record about these new friends was that Nimet Cattaoui's parents were part of the ruling Establishment of Egypt. They were an elegant, sophisticated couple, René Cattaoui sporting the Legion d'Honneur red rosette in his buttonhole. Although both Orthodox Jews, René Cattaoui was a Senator in the Egyptian Senate, while his wife was Lady-in-Waiting to Queen Farida. Such a concept seems like a fantasy these days, but there was then, and had been for some years, a section of the Jewish community in Egypt that was both rich and influential. An ancestor of René Cattaoui's is mentioned in Ahdef Souief's *Map of Love* as having been a member of the Egyptian Establishment at the turn of the twentieth century.

I never saw Desmond O'Meara again nor the Smouhas, but Nimet and I met frequently at the Club once we returned to Cairo.

We now lived in an attractive, if small, flat on Sharia el Gezira, overlooking the Club. Within a few weeks we were to move to a much larger flat on the corner of Sharia Fuad el Awal, with the Gezira Preparatory School opposite the side road and the Egyptians Officers' Club across the main road. We now had to get used to the roar of the traffic from the latter: the rattling of the trams and the constant sound of motor horns (so great a nuisance were these to become that Nasser was in the future to ban their use). Each morning I would make my way to the Lido, where I met old friends from childhood and made new ones. As in childhood, we were a cosmopolitan lot. The Vernon Jarvis girls' mother was Italian, Minnie Wilkinson and Maurice Constant had Syrian mothers, Tené was a Swede, Nimet Cattaoui, Gamila Green and the Ades girls were Egyptian Jews. And our group included a couple of Egyptian boys as well as a few English girls fresh from boarding school.

They admitted me quickly into their circle and soon I was part of a swirling social life. Too late in the season for swimming, we played tennis and went roller-skating. We went to the pictures and to parties in one another's homes (although not ours). It was delightful to be welcomed so readily and I was having a good time, in spite of the fact that those of us who had been to boarding school in England were plump from too much school starch and were socially a little gauche. The girls who had stayed behind at school in Cairo seemed elegant and sophisticated by comparison. One or two of them were stunningly beautiful. Most of all I envied their relaxed self-assurance. Nevertheless, I had an admirer. Maurice Constant, with whom I shared a passion for P.G. Wodehouse, became very attentive and we had some good times together. But, as his father said to mine, 'Maurice flits from flower to flower' and after some weeks he became interested in another member of the group.

The war seemed far away, although by degrees our childhood friends joined up and would appear at the Club in uniform: David Ades who went into the Signals and one of whose fellow officers was to marry his sister, Jeanie; Lionel Saxby, slim and handsome in RAF blue, who was to be killed within weeks of going into the desert; Eric Vernon Jarvis who fought throughout the war, only to be killed a few weeks before VE Day, leaving a widow and two children; merry Raymond Shorten was to join Popski's Private Army, a rogue group of raiding soldiers under the command of a Belgian/Pole, Captain Peniakoff, which wreaked havoc on the German lines in the Western Desert. Raymond was to die at Tobruk.

But those griefs were ahead of us. It was the time of the Phoney War when, having conquered Poland, the Germans ceased activity. For these quiet months both sides in the conflict were building up their forces.

And in the meantime, in Cairo we played. As well as enjoying life with my contemporaries, there were drinks parties and dinners that I went to with my parents.

But underlying the frivolity there was melancholy. I often wept out of nostalgia for England and Mollie and the old life with the Llewellyns, even for Cambridge. My relationship with Joan didn't improve. Scrawled across my diary are the eternal words of the teenager: *'I can't do anything right and I'm sick of it!'*

Much more importantly, my father was in financial difficulties. On the outbreak of war, advertising in *The Sphinx* had dried up and without advertising no magazine can survive. His sub-editor, who had been running the paper all summer, believed it would have to go bankrupt. Having announced this bombshell one night at dinner, he resigned from his job the next day. My father seriously considered putting the paper into receivership.

But most of his income came from the salary he paid himself from *The Sphinx*. Otherwise he received a small retaining fee from the *Telegraph,* the *Mail* and Exchange Telegraph and was paid for any stories of his that they published. This money went into his London bank account to be used on holidays or towards his old age. He investigated the possibility of a job with the newly established censorship, but all the posts had by then been filled by a variety of Cairo businessmen. It was unlikely he would get other work now that he was in his sixties.

We were never as well off as we might have been because my father stubbornly refused to claim expenses. I've never understood quite why. High-mindedness? Because he could always manage very well, thank you very much? Or because he always had a horror of discussing money? I have a memory of Malcolm Muggeridge, an old friend and in Cairo on behalf of the *Telegraph* (and probably also working for MI6) perched on the arm of a chair at the Continental Hotel trying to persuade my father to claim expenses from London.

After the war Malcolm was to do my father a good turn in this respect. By then he was deputy editor of the *Telegraph* and he managed to persuade the board to give my father a small pension.

We were facing a crisis. Economy was the order of the day. No phone calls unless they were urgent. No indulgences like taxis. My school trunk full of clothes had been sent by long sea voyage and didn't arrive for weeks. In the meantime I had very few clothes and no money could be spent on new ones. Joan tried to alter her old clothes for me and I remember the shame of playing tennis with Jeanie Ades in a tussore V-necked dress in the style of the twenties. (In those days it was *de rigueur* to wear white for tennis. I wouldn't have dreamt of wearing an ordinary cotton dress.)

Eventually, two solutions proposed themselves. My father, through personal contacts, got back most of the advertising for *The Sphinx* and decided to adapt it to appeal more to servicemen.

Secondly, I had to get a job.

Work . . .

So, at sixteen, I got my first job in the typing pool of the Anglo-Egyptian Censorship. I was paid £6 a month, of which I gave half to Joan for my keep.

The Censorship was housed on one floor of the Shell building in central Cairo. The typing pool consisted of about fifteen of us herded together in a windowless dark room. The other girls were all Egyptian or held British passports, but the latter were Maltese or Cypriot or had Greek or Egyptian mothers. They were warm and friendly and welcomed me in. We had one male member of the pool: Ches, a handsome young American putting in his gap year before going to university in the States. He was a cheerful young man and would entertain us to stories and flirt affectionately with the young girls. He even went so far as to arrange outings for us. A trip on a *felucca* is the one I remember.

Not having good shorthand, I was given copy-typing, which I had learnt at school. Day after day I typed reports from the Alexandria Cotton Exchange. Cotton was Egypt's main export at the time, but I have never known what this had to do with censorship and the work was unutterably boring. It was also stressful as I didn't understand a word I was typing.

But it was a job and I felt proud to be going out to work in the new outfit Joan had invested in: a dark brown sweater and a knobbly brown woollen skirt.

Before long I had been spotted by Mrs. Johnson Brown who ran the Central Registry in a corner of the typing pool with the help of two other women. She applied to have me added to her staff and I was transferred.

Another boring job, that of Despatch Clerk, which consisted of entering all the letters in a ledger, stamping with sealing wax the top secret ones and handing them all over to the dispatch rider five times a day for delivery.

But this time I was to be highly entertained. Mrs. Johnson Brown (Mrs. J-B) was the wife of a Regular Army colonel and the other two women, Vi Clarke and Nancy Orr, were also Regular Army wives. The gossip while we worked never ceased. I learnt a great many insights into married life and into pre-war regimental life and the wives' welfare work among "their men". I also learnt about Army snobbery. Class distinction was a fact of life among the middle classes in those days and I had been well schooled in snobbery by the girls at the Convent and by my mother. I reckoned I could place to a T someone's background by their accent, use of words, body language and clothes. In the Army the class lines were rigid. Mrs. J-B came near the bottom of the social scale as her husband was in the Royal Ordnance Corps. But Mrs. J-B was saved by the fact that her husband was a colonel and that they both had become experts in desert terrain. Most weekends before the war and in the earliest days they would explore further into the desert and camp out.

In any case Mrs. J-B's sense of her own importance was irrepressible. She had worked in the Central Registry of the War Office and considered she knew it all and that in her absence everything would collapse (she was later to test this out). Her appearance matched her personality: bony and bow-legged, she had a beaky, acne-covered face, protuberant blue eyes behind pince-nez and blonde hair tightly scrolled in corkscrew curls. She hooted and harrumphed her way through each day and we were in thrall to her.

Nancy Orr's husband was also in the RAOC, but she had a quiet self-confidence born of boundless good humour and a happy marriage. She was a plump and jolly blonde and nothing unsettled her.

The third Army officer wife was Vi Clarke, married to a Cavalry major, near the top of the social hierarchy. She was very conscious of this and was often unconvincingly to decry its importance. But she was an endearing small, pretty woman, witty and amusing, and she took a protective interest in me.

It was when we moved offices that Mrs. J-B made her dramatic gesture. We moved to a large modern building on the Corniche between the Bulaq Bridge and the Anglican Cathedral. Our office was large with a beautiful view over the Nile: *dahabiyehs* (houseboats) lining the banks of the river and a palm tree-fringed horizon with the tiny triangles of the Pyramids in the far, far distance. Then, the most spectacular sunsets in the world. The Censorship occupied the whole of the building and the floor above ours housed the laboratory in which presumably letters were tested for secret writing, etc. It was headed by our friend, Eric Titterington, who had been head pharmacist to King Faruk and who now was elevated to Major. The other department heads were all Cairo businessmen who had also automatically gone into Army uniform.

The day we moved offices, Mrs. J-B walked out.

Her new desk wasn't big enough!

For several days, Colonel MacLean, the Chief Censor, refused to give way. Mr. Grant, one of the office orderlies, was roped in to take her place. He was a retired Regular Army Sergeant who had married an Egyptian girl and remained on in Cairo after his service in the Middle East. Quietly and modestly he sat at Mrs. J-B's (not-big-enough) desk, presumably doing her work well enough. We equally quietly, subdued by the turn of events, got on with ours. After several days, a large desk was suddenly produced and Mrs. J-B harrumphed her way back.

She was unstoppable after this. She was constantly waging war with other departments and most of all with Colonel MacLean. She would disappear for a while and then return, bow legs flashing, corkscrew curls bobbing. 'Hah!' she would cry. 'Hoist with his own petard!' She would then sit down and regale us with details of her latest victory.

Soon we were joined by two more Regular Army wives, Rosanna Yates (Cavalry – very posh) and Mrs. Graham (Indian Army – *sans reproche),* a plump, middle aged mother figure.

Then there was "Hammy". Major Hamilton occupied a corner of our large room, hidden behind a sort of hospital screen. His tall lugubrious figure would appear at the beginning of the day and remain hidden until the end. He walked to work from Gezira and as soon as he arrived and was hidden behind the screen, a shirt, stained with sweat, would be flung over the screen, while Hammy put on a clean one. His job was to give a final check to all the telegrams for hidden codes but he never gave any evidence that he had found any. Our constant chatter must have maddened him.

Cairo was by now, allegedly, swarming with spies and secret agents. Most German and Italians had been interned, but mysteriously there still remained a great many enemy civilians at large and letters and cables had to be rigorously examined. One of the minor scandals of the time was that Lily, my father's former secretary and now married to an Italian (who was not interned) was secretary to the Hon. Cecil Campbell (he insisted on the Hon!), head of Marconi and in charge of cable censorship. (In fact she later left her husband and became his mistress. I was saddened by this because I had adored her as a child and she never seemed happy with Cecil Campbell. He eventually committed suicide but he did leave her comfortably off and she and the Gavazis retired to Italy after the war.)

Apart from Hammy, all the top-secret work in our building was done in other departments. We never saw anything of the slightest interest and I have since wondered why it needed five women to keep non-secret files. What on earth could have been in them?

Our move to the new premises was noteworthy for another event. Charlie, the despatch rider, stole a kiss from me. But that's for another chapter.

By the beginning of 1941 the war was going extremely badly for the Allies. As well as his pre-war conquests, Hitler had occupied Denmark, Norway, the Netherlands and France. Russia and Italy were now his allies and the latter was moving into the Balkans towards Greece as well as fighting our troops in the Western Desert with a view to occupying Egypt. Malta was being subjected to a blitz equal in ferocity with the London blitz and the Maltese people were collectively to earn the award of the George Cross, awarded for civilian bravery. (The correct way to address Malta is Malta, G.C.). Donald took part in the battle of Malta. He once described how relentless it had been. The Spitfire pilots fought their battles in the air, landed exhausted, fell asleep in their chairs and before they felt anything like refreshed were up in the air again taking part in another battle.

The Mediterranean was now becoming a dangerous hot spot, with the result that two people important to our family left Egypt for the safety of South Africa.

The first to do so was Joan's chest specialist and his departure had a disastrous effect on Joan's health. It's important at this stage to talk of her illness, which was severe and which for the next two years was to be a worrying and threatening accompaniment to the lives of my father and myself.

Dr. Schwarz was a Swiss, living in Alexandria, and every fortnight after we arrived in Egypt I would accompany Joan there so that he could re-inflate the tubercular lung that had been collapsed in England before the war. This procedure had kept her going. She was a semi-invalid, but could lead a fairly normal life, playing bridge with her teacher friends from P.I., entertaining people to lunch or dinner. She had, after all, no housework or cooking or shopping to do. The sum total of her daily housekeeping was to interview Abdul the cook each evening to hear his account of how he had spent his daily allowance of fifteen piastres in the market and to give him his instructions for the next day. I took over this duty when Joan was too ill and the procedure took only a few minutes.

After Dr. Schwarz's departure Joan transferred to Dr. Cherif, the only chest specialist of repute in Cairo. He was a caring and competent man, but he did not know how to re-inflate her lung. She became ill, first with quinsy, then with a sudden onset of severe rheumatoid arthritis. Finally her lung became reinfected. This must have been a recurrence of active TB, but the word was never used to me. Only once, after some months, did Dr. Cherif casually say that she should have her own crockery and cutlery.

Joan was to become bedridden for nearly two years. At her worst she went down to five stone in weight and couldn't move her arms at all, so that she had to be dressed, washed and fed. Once her lung had become infected, Dr. Cherif would visit her to draw off the fluid, full of pus and blood, with a menacing-looking syringe, which he plunged through her ribcage. Joan would grasp my hands during this procedure, tightly, tightly.

We had a series of carers to look after her. The first was a woman of indeterminate nationality who lived with a large extended family on a *dahabiyeh* on the Nile and who was so poor, she said, that she wore the same clothes until they fell off her. I certainly never knew her to wear anything different. She was kind and fairly competent, but was soon replaced by another woman, also of indeterminate nationality. She was a fussy little woman with a squint, whose one idea of curing Joan was to ply her with *piqures.* Joan resisted these injections forcibly and I'm not sure what was supposed to be in them.

Then we had the only qualified nurse to look after Joan – "Sister Francis", a Frenchwoman who gave her devoted attention. She lived in, sleeping in my room while I slept on a sofa in the drawing room. (When we had only daily carers I looked after Joan at night with the help of a Heath Robinson arrangement of strings and a bell in my bedroom. If Joan rang in the night, I would wake up on my feet in alarm. I had one night off a week and would settle Joan down for the night and leave her alone for a couple of hours to go to choir rehearsal. My father always worked late into the night.)

Sister was a strong character and an intelligent woman, but she had a few large chips on her shoulder. It must, I realise, have been difficult to be a citizen of a country which had surrendered to the enemy. A large area of France colluded with the enemy, with Marshal Petain as its President. She planned to return to work with children as soon as France had been liberated. She worked hard and long hours with us. At the end of her day, she would soak her feet in a mustard bath and sit grumbling to me while eating the pound block of fruit and nut chocolate I had bought for her at l'Americaine. She hated men, my father in particular, for coming home late from the Turf Club and going in to talk over the day's affairs with Joan. She had no understanding that it was at the club that my father picked up his most important political and social news. Nor that his nightly visits to his wife may have been what kept her interest in life alive.

She also thought it scandalous that I should dutifully look after Joan on her off-duty and tried to raise the rebel in me. She succeeded in so far as I once went off for the whole day without saying where I was (at the pictures!). But I never repeated the experiment.

Sister taught me a lesson in professionalism that I've never forgotten. She was sitting as usual, feet in bowl of hot water, grumbling about the heavy demands made on her by Joan when the latter rang her bell. Muttering a curse, Sister shuffled on her slippers and we both went to Joan's room. The moment we entered Sister was all gentle solicitude, soothing Joan and making her as comfortable as possible. Not a hint of the ungracious complaining woman of a minute before. I was impressed.

After Sister left, we had Frieda, a stolid plain German girl who had escaped internment. She was very good to Joan, while being young and inexperienced. She contracted diphtheria at one stage and had to be temporarily replaced (I can't remember by whom), but she came back and stayed with us after Joan's partial recovery, as a companion. We became very fond of her. I have always felt a bit guilty about Frieda's diphtheria because soon afterwards I was found to be a carrier and must have infected her. I had to be admitted to the same fever hospital on the outskirts of Cairo. With Egyptian doctors and an English matron, the care was adequate and in any case I didn't feel ill.

Joan had few visitors. Severe illness frightens people off. Vi Bramble, who lived next door called in frequently, as did Mootie de Knevett, who was probably Joan's best friend. A large domineering woman, both of whose arms jangled from wrist to elbow with silver bangles from the Muski, she was very fond of Joan and took a motherly interest in her. A less frequent visitor was Peggy Titterington, who would rush in with a large workbag and sit and regale Joan with all the latest gossip while knitting or sewing "comforts" for the troops. Then off she would rush – 'Tea with the Bishop, dear' or 'Quartet tonight!' (she played the violin). 'Must go home and prepare.' She always cheered Joan up. At Mootie's instigation, Father Leonard, a Franciscan from St. Joseph's Cathedral, visited her also and soon Joan was received back into the Catholic Church and was to derive great comfort from this.

But Joan did have a companion who delighted her – Richard the lizard, who would appear from a corner in the ceiling and dart around snapping at real or imaginary insects. He was a beautiful little creature and gave her great pleasure. It led my father to hit on the idea of getting her a canary. After a visit to the most remarkable bird shop in central Cairo – three floors of cages full of birds chattering and twittering – we came home with a Prince Canary. He was a rare type, almost white in colour with a crown of black feathers. He sang beautifully and Joan fell in love with him and called him Pip. We dated the start of her slow recovery from the day we brought Pip home.

Joan had three bouts of hospitalisation. The first was in the German Hospital in central Cairo, run by the German Deaconesses, who by virtue of their religious profession had escaped internment. (The Italian Roman Catholic convent and church on Gezira also escaped and were regarded with great suspicion by the Censorship.) While in the German Hospital Joan nearly died. She was to tell the story of how, when she was at her worst, she saw a group of nuns at the end of her bed praying. Later she asked who they had been and was told by the ward sister that there had been no visitors but that the Carmelite nuns had been asked to pray for her.

Some time later, in despair I suspect, Dr. Cherif suggested she go to the TB sanatorium in Helwan, the health resort where I had been at boarding school. My father and I went to visit her when she had been there a week, to find her very unhappy. There was a nest of bugs behind her headboard. Ambulant patients were apt to spit on the floor of the corridors.

My father made an appeal to our very good friend, Rosa Sayer, the Swiss wife of a Cairo business man, who was unbelievably kind to us as a family throughout those trying times. She found a Swiss family in Helwan who were happy to have Joan for a sort of convalescent period. They were a delightful family, warm and friendly and Madame was an expert cook. With the fresh air of Helwan and good Swiss food, Joan began to put on weight and look better. But soon after her return home to Cairo she had another relapse.

The third hospital to be tried was a hospital in Alexandria. In the Autumn of 1942 I went to visit her and while we were talking we became aware of a constant rumbling as of thunder. We were hearing the guns of el Alamein. This was the battle which was to turn the tide of the war in our favour.

Soon after my visit, Joan went down with pneumonia. Then an apparent miracle happened. There was still no cure for this illness other than skilled nursing, which she received. When she came out of the pneumonia, the rheumatoid arthritis had completely disappeared. She was never to have another twinge. The infection in her lung also cleared in time, although the lung was still collapsed and useless and had pushed her heart slightly out of place. When Joan returned from Alexandria I came home from work to find her holding court in her room with my father, Rosa Sayer and Mootie de Knevett. She suddenly got up from her chair to walk to her bed and I panicked. I hadn't seen her walk for over two years.

Joan's recovery coincided with the recovery of our fortunes in the war and by degrees we were to feel the relief of this. The grinding anxiety about the possibility of defeat and the constant, constant concern about Joan were both lifted.

The other person who had taken fright at the way the war was going and who had fled to South Africa was Mrs. Cunliffe, my father's secretary. He asked me if I would leave the Censorship and work on *The Sphinx* with him.

At last I had a job that I could enjoy for itself.

The Sphinx came out weekly, on a Saturday, and was probably read as much for the society news as anything. My father wrote these pages which were not only about the Court, the diplomats, the VIPs, so many of whom came to Cairo during the war, but also about the receptions, the parties, the weddings, the deaths of the English middle class community. As the desert wars progressed he added the deaths of men who had been killed in battle, obituaries gleaned from the London *Times*.

But there was much more to *The Sphinx* than that. The political leader at the front was written by Harold Earle, editor of *The Egyptian Gazette,* and it was usually followed by one or two original articles of topical interest. The best reading during the war was the weekly London Letter, written by our friend Philip O'Farrell, a journalist who gave a brilliant, personal account of London life in the war – particularly vivid during the Blitz. The centre pages were called Mainly About People, the social news. The back section contained the sports, arts and book reviews, written by local contributors. The Woman's Page and Crossword were syndicated out from London.

The Sphinx Publishing Company occupied a square, single storey building, with cellar underneath, probably housing the newsprint. Our offices were on the left-hand side of a small flight of stairs to the central front door. Max Fischer and *The Egyptian Directory* were to the right. To the side of the building were our printing works. (We were gratified, my father and I that, when at school I'd visited the Oxford University Press, I'd found that their printing presses weren't as modern as ours.)

We were a small staff. My father and I, the only members of the editorial staff, shared one large room to the front. Behind us, in another large room, were Mr. Aboaf, a Jugoslav accountant, Dmitri (Greek), who drummed up and negotiated the small advertisements (my father got the main ads from the big companies through his personal contacts) and Osman, the office boy and messenger.

As soon as my father arrived at the office he reverted to journalist type. The Savile Row-dressed, dapper man in jaunty trilby and monocle disappeared. His jacket and hat were hung up, his sleeves rolled up and he would light a cigarette and chain-smoke his way through the day's work. If he found no cigarettes in his drawer he would pace up and down impotently until Osman had returned from the shop with packets of Players. He typed all his own letters and copy, rattling away at the typewriter by his desk.

Having been strictly instructed by my father, my main job was proof-reading. The printers were all Egyptian and in spite of the fact that their standards of typesetting were high, we had at least two galleys of everything. My father pasted up the pages and always read the final proofs. I also selected the crossword winner, wrote it up and sent off the prize book token. I was in charge of the petty cash and Dmitri would go off on his weekly rounds to collect the money for the small ads he had negotiated. He then handed over the money to me when I checked the receipts. There were always one or two who "hadn't paid". I raised this with my father. 'Don't worry,' he said. 'That money is Dmitri's perk. Don't question it too much.'

Soon I was contributing to *The Sphinx*. I wrote a weekly page: Hollywood Notes, by Pete (Mollie's nickname for me). This meant collecting the publicity for forthcoming films from MGM and Twentieth Century Fox and knocking it into a page of gossip about the film stars. As you can imagine the page had a regular readership. I also wrote the occasional article. I remember one about a Cairo child's Christmas; one about a holiday in Luxor when we stayed at the Winter Palace; another an interview with Clifford Harker, who was going to conduct the first ever performance in Egypt of Handel's *Messiah*.

We worked each day from nine until one o'clock when my father repaired to the Turf Club round the corner for a drink and I went home. Lunch was at two o'clock when my father had got home, followed by a siesta. The servants were free after lunch until the evening, so I got tea for us and we worked again at the office from four until seven.

As the war intensified in the Middle East, we began to go to press conferences and this routine was interrupted.

The conferences were held at one o'clock every day, first in Garden City and then in the Immobilia Building in central Cairo. They lasted an hour, most of which was off the record information, not for publication. Towards the end we were handed the official communiqué. My father would type this out, together with his comments – a different cable for each of the papers he represented – and my job was to rush them to the press censor.

The Middle East, after the fall of France in 1940, became the centre of military operations. GHQ Middle East, who had taken over the Semiramis Hotel, were responsible for operations from Tunisia in the West, the whole of north Africa, Egypt, Palestine, Greece, Malta. The Italians invaded North Africa with the intention of taking Egypt with its access to the Suez Canal and the oil fields of the Gulf. The Germans to start with concentrated on the northern Mediterranean – Malta and Greece.

Because of the importance of the area, all the big beasts from Fleet Street were sent to Cairo – Richard Dimbleby, Alan Moorehead, Alexander Clifford, Clare Hollingsworth, Noel Barber and others, all of whom were household names at the time. They, of course, covered the war in the field, but their base was Cairo. Hence the press conferences. They usually gathered together in the uniforms of the official War Correspondent, green tabs on their shoulders. Richard Dimbleby's large bulk filled the same window each day. (It was said that the way to his heart was to ask after his small son, David.)

That hour each day was fascinating, because the information we were given was top secret and we knew exactly how the war was going – and it was not going well for us most of the time. During 1941 the battles raged back and forth in the desert. There seemed no reason why they should ever be resolved. Eventually, although the British were outnumbered by the Italians eight to one, we pushed them back to Tunisia. It had always been said that the "Ities" hadn't the stomach for the fight and they suddenly gave themselves up in shoals. There was the famous despatch sent by a Tank Commander to headquarters: 'For God's sake send in the infantry. We're surrounded by prisoners.'

At first the Press Officer in charge of the conference was Philip Astley, handsome in colonel's uniform and also with an aura of glamour because he was married to Madeleine Carroll, a film star of the day. After a while, he was replaced by Winston Churchill's son, Randolph. His first day they stood on the platform together, Randolph surveying the room. His eyes, bright blue, alighted on me and I saw him ask who I was. Having been told, I saw his lips: 'Out!' Quite rightly he considered me a security risk. I was only seventeen, and in a short cotton dress with my hair falling round my shoulders, must have looked quite irresponsible. It would never have occurred to me to divulge anything I had heard in a conference, but out I had to go. I would wait in the corridor until the conference was over and then run with my father's cables to the censor's office.

I was always fascinated by cablese. The cost of a cable was charged according to the number of words, so the press had a way of cutting this down, by the use of Latin. A message to say "A battalion of the Scots Guards, together with a unit of the Royal Tank Corps, advanced to Sidi Bahrein . . .' would read 'Battalion Scotsguards cumunit Royaltankcorps advanced adSidiBahrein . . .' This would be easy enough, but I wondered how journalists managed to transcribe elegant prose into this jargon.

After the conference we often stayed in town to lunch, my father introducing the journalists from England to local Syrian and Egyptian restaurants. Or my father would eat at the Turf Club while I had sandwiches in the Ladies Room, or I'd wander into town to eat at l'Americaine where you could get good coffee and Swiss pastries at half the cost of the famous Groppi's.

When Joan had recovered from her illness, we had open house on Sundays, when my father would bring home two or three war correspondents for lunch; often they stayed on to tea. The conversation flowed and it was invariably fascinating. I realised my great good luck in meeting these intelligent, witty men so informally, but I'm afraid I remember no interesting stories to tell about them.

My eighteenth birthday arrived and I became liable for military service. I longed to join the Wrens, the women's branch of the Royal Navy and considered by me to be the elite of the women's services. But Joan was still seriously ill and it felt like desertion to leave her and my father. The alternative was to find civilian war work.

My father heard that the Ministry of Information, newly established in Cairo, were looking for a layout girl. I applied and got the job. We reached a compromise which satisfied the authorities: that I should work for three days a week with my father, one day of which incorporated Friday, the day the paper "went to bed". The other three days were to be at the MOI.

(All through the war we worked six days a week and I didn't get a holiday until January 1943, three and a half years after the war's outbreak. Then I had an unforgettable fortnight in Luxor and two more week-long holidays were to follow, later in 1943 and 1944, both in Alexandria. I used to hear with envy of girl-friends who managed to get "lifts" in RAF planes to Cyprus or Palestine, but I never managed anything like that!)

The MOI was at first housed in Garden City near the British Embassy, with whose publicity department in the shape of Lawrence Durrell we had close links. Larry was handsome in a Churchillian way at that time and known mainly as a poet. Our immediate boss, Sue Southby, admired him but she once had the temerity to tell him she didn't understand his poetry. 'No,' he replied, 'but it sounds pretty, don't you think?' Our department at the MOI was responsible for bringing out propaganda magazines stating the British view of the war to the Arabs, the Greeks and the Turks. *Al Akhbar* (The War) was circulated throughout all the Arab countries. *AEPA* was circulated to Greek soldiers serving in Egypt and was dropped by parachute over German-occupied Greece. *Cephe* was circulated in Turkey, a neutral country, important because she was wedged between German-occupied Europe and the Allied-occupied eastern Mediterranean. The latter magazine was our pride and more money was poured into it than into the other two, particularly as it was in direct competition with a German propaganda magazine. The comparatively new process of printing by rotogravure had reached Egypt and all our three journals were to concentrate on pictorial presentation. This was obligatory with *Cephe* as the Turkish government had stipulated that magazines from both Britain and Germany should only have so many words per page. *AEPA* had mainly text, but *Al Akhbar* relied to a large extent on pictures.

Soon we moved to larger offices between the Anglican Cathedral and Groppi's Rotunda. It was a tall building on a traffic island between three main roads and as well as the MOI staff on the top floor, it also housed the editorial staff of several service papers and magazines. A former sub-editor of my father's, Harold Rushton, had now been elevated to colonel status and edited *Parade,* based on *Picture Post.* My friend Roy Nash edited *Gen,* an entertaining and stimulating pocket magazine of the sort fashionable at the time. Apart from Harold, all the editorial staff of the service press were journalists who had joined up but were now seconded to providing information and entertainment for the troops.

We were all supported by a fleet of secretaries (civilian) and orderlies (servicemen) and by both photograph and general libraries (Elizabeth Gwynne – later to become Elizabeth David, the famous cookery writer – worked in the latter. A plain unhappy-looking girl I thought her. It was rumoured around that she had Indian blood.) On the floor below us was a NAAFI canteen and we subsisted on strong black tea, which I still love. The orderlies lived on the roof, presumably in cell-like rooms. (Just as it never occurred to me to enquire into the living conditions of our servants on our apartment roofs, so I didn't think to enquire how our personal orderlies, Privates Peacock and Mackie, fared up there.) Next to our office were large studios for the artists. Sevek, a mid-European Jew, was our office clown and entirely endearing. He started a portrait of me in oils to show at an exhibition planned of his work. But I childishly got fed up with spending precious Sunday mornings posing for him and stopped attending the sessions. The portrait was turned to the wall.

Our three magazines had a Greek, a Turk and an Egyptian as translators and we had two editors. Roger Eland, more large amiable puppy than serious grown-up, edited *AEPA* and *Cephe*. He must have had flair, for both publications were very successful. By contrast Jim Stewart, older than Roger, highly intelligent, taciturn, edited *Al Akhbar*. He had been editor of *The Architectural Review* together with John Betjeman before the war and, probably because I was young and biddable, I was his favourite layout girl. He had demanding standards and he taught me how to lay out a page to best effect, to look for the beauty in a photograph, how to trim it to maximum advantage.

(After the war he was to become a household name. The one and only arts review programme broadcast in the forties and fifties was "The Critics" on the radio's Third Programme. Jim was the arts critic and week after week he would be heard pronouncing on the latest art exhibition. In his later years he was knighted.)

There were four of us in our office. Sue Southby lounged gracefully in the far end of the long room. She made the fashion pages her particular interest and, being an artist, often illustrated them herself. At the other end of the room was Anne Williams, divorced from a member of the PI and with an only son with grandparents in England. She had a dry wit and was enjoying the social life that wartime Cairo offered a single woman. Opposite me at our large desk in the middle was Olive Stewart, nicknamed Olive because of her resemblance to Olive Oyl, Popeye's wife in the cartoons.

Married to a lecturer at Cairo University, now serving with the RAF, she was a modest warm person, of whom I became very fond. She and her husband were both Socialists and subscribed to the Left Book Club, copies of which she would sometimes lend me. They were passionately in favour of the independence of Egypt and they are the couple I have referred to before who were to be tragically killed and disembowelled in the Cairo riots of 1952.

As well as working on *Al Akhbar* I was allocated the job of being responsible for "Glamour" and "Sport" for *Cephe*. We would be sent out packets of photographs from London, but if there was no suitable story in them for Glamour, I would visit my old friends at MGM and 20th Century Fox and collect some material. I would take the sports photographs that came from London to the *Gazette* offices to get captions from their sports editor. He was another Fleet Street journalist in uniform who had been seconded to journalism. The circulation of the English-speaking papers must have soared during the war with so many servicemen pouring into Egypt and nothing but the best was considered necessary for them. Certainly this chap knew his sport and would respond excitedly to the photographs I brought him.

I stayed at the MOI until I left for England in March 1945 to get married. I had enjoyed working there, met interesting people and had learnt some good basic skills, in addition to those I had learnt at *The Sphinx*. Roger and Jim offered to give me references and put me in touch with London colleagues, but with the airy confidence of youth I turned their offers down. I foresaw my future as a wife.

Once of the more bizarre incidents that I experienced during the war was when I was at the MOI.

An RAF sergeant had stayed late one night to write a letter home to his wife when he was murdered –his throat slit – and the contents of the office safe emptied. The military CID poured in to investigate and we all had our fingerprints taken. It was almost certainly an inside job as the night security was tight. We wondered if one of our orderlies had been responsible. He was a tough little man from the Gorbals in Glasgow, where it was known razor gangs had been rife before the war. But the CID were never able to make an arrest.

We had just had our fingerprints taken and someone was commenting on how awful it would be if one's prints were found to be incriminating and yet one were innocent. On cue (and my memory tells me this literally happened), Peacock entered the room and said: 'Miss Taylor, the CID want to speak to you.'

However it was about a quite different case. A CID Sergeant was waiting for me. He told me that the Egyptian police were holding a young man accused of some minor offence who was in fact believed to be a deserter from the Royal Navy. He had given my name as a reference. I was shown his photograph and a list of aliases that he was believed to have used. I was mystified. By this stage of the war I had met literally hundreds of servicemen at dances, parties, clubs, in the street. I couldn't make out who he was. Would I accompany the sergeant to the police station? I got permission and in a few minutes was riding thrillingly at great speed in the back of an open police jeep. At Cairo's main police station we ploughed through Arabs squatting on the floor of the corridors and were ushered into the presence of a police officer.

The young man was brought in and immediately I felt a great pity for him. He looked so forlorn and was gazing at me pleadingly, but I didn't know who on earth he was. He refused to speak and help me out and the Egyptian officer refused to let me see him alone as suggested by the CID sergeant. So we had to give up and go home.

When I got home I found a letter had arrived from him: a letter telling me he dreamed of me every night. Something in the letter gave me a clue and I remembered. Some months before, this young man had turned up at home asking to see my father in the hope of getting a job. My father was still out, Joan would have nothing to do with him, so I sat and talked to him – possibly the first courtesy he had received in a while. When my father returned he got short shrift and was sent away without a job – but we were to discover later that he probably did have a photograph of me that had been on the hall table. I phoned the CID to report and I thought that was the last I'd hear of the case.

But some weeks later I met the CID sergeant in the street. 'Your young man –' he said, 'He was proved to be a deserter from the Navy. You will be interested to hear that while he was being taken under escort to Alexandria to be court-marshalled he escaped.' He grinned and passed on his way.

Meanwhile at *The Sphinx* my father was having more trouble. The demand for newsprint due to the influx of so many servicemen resulted in a severe shortage. Whether the price shot up so that it was more than my father could manage, or whether priority was given to official departments and the daily papers, I don't remember. Whatever the reason our supply of newsprint was fast drying up and my father had to sell out to the SOP (Société Orientale de Publicité) who owned the two English dailies, *Al Ahram* and the French daily, *Le Bourse.*

We left our picturesque offices for a suite of rooms in central Cairo and then, with reduced staff, for the main building of the SOP. Our staff now consisted of myself, my father and a rather dim middle-aged Coptic office boy. The SOP were to handle our finance and advertising.

In 1943 my father got his first week's holiday of the war, going to Mena House. For that week *The Sphinx* was brought out by myself and a young New Zealand sergeant, a journalist on the NZ forces' paper, who spent his week's leave to help out. After my father's feverish attack on work, John Spedding was delightfully relaxed. He brought cookies his mother had sent him to the office and would come and sit by my desk and chat. We became good friends and were to enjoy many outings together.

About a year before I left Egypt I went to work at the MOI full time and I can't remember how my father managed after that.

(When the war ended and the British presence largely evaporated, *The Sphinx* sadly dwindled to a few paragraphs in the *Gazette*. Undaunted, and in his late sixties, my father took on the job of managing editor of a new London-funded journal, *Anglo-Arab Trade,* which he edited until my parents came home to England permanently in 1953.

This was after the revolution when the King and his family were banished from the country and the Revolutionary Council had taken over. The British – and other foreign nationals, maybe, I don't know – had to leave and my parents were unable to bring out any money or possessions other than their clothes. Thanks to my father's savings over the years deposited in London and thanks to the small pension wangled for him by Malcolm Muggeridge, by then the deputy editor of *The Daily Telegraph,* they managed financially, but in comparative poverty.)

. . . and Play

It is daunting to have to describe what Cairo was like during the Second World War. Books have been written about the subject and here we have only a few paragraphs.

To begin with life for the British, Cairo-style, continued as usual, except that some of the younger men joined up in the services and some of the older men rushed into uniform in such jobs as the Censorship. The women continued to run their homes, go to the Club and to bridge parties and to coffee at Groppi's and to each other's cocktail parties. The Army continued to play cricket and polo at the club, and senior staff officers rode as usual to BTE (HQ British Troops in Egypt) in their staff cars. The latter practice came to an end after Churchill visited Egypt in 1941 and was shocked by the general waste of resources. After that staff officers under the rank of general had to travel in communal lorries or make their own way to and from work. (Such lorries conveyed home those of us at the MOI who lived in Gezira or Heliopolis. My two memories of those rides are of the glorious vivid sunsets over the Nile and the less pleasing one of catching the fleas that leapt on to my bare legs the moment I boarded. During the day the lorry would have been used for conveying goods and bales of newsprint in which the fleas would nest.)

The teenagers continued to meet at the Club, play tennis, go to the cinema and to parties in each other's homes. This was my life during the first weeks of the war. And I suffered the usual teenage agonies: hearing one boy say to another at a party as I danced by in my new long evening dress: 'Who's that fat girl in green?' Etc. . .

The city of Cairo also carried on as normal on the surface, except that martial law was declared in Egypt, placing all communications at Britain's disposal and establishing the censorship. Germans were interned. The Embassy conducted a census and were shocked to find so many elderly English widows living in poverty. After their husbands had died they had decided to stay on in Egypt and were now destitute, living on the charity of their Arab neighbours. They were offered repatriation.

On the surface nothing changed and the Cairo streets pulsated with life as usual. Then into Cairo's cosmopolitan maelstrom poured the Allied troops. In the autumn of 1940, there were only a few thousand of them. Within six months they numbered over 35,000. By degrees they were joined by Allied troops from all over the world. The streets literally swarmed with khaki: British tommies, in their long crumpled shorts, still pale from England, looking bewildered and in awe of this alien country; Indian soldiers, handsome and graceful; South Africans, blonde and blue-eyed, with their long, long bronzed legs in their short, short shorts; New Zealanders, crowded into gharries careering round the city and ostentatiously feeding the under-nourished horses. The Free French, the Belgians and the Poles arrived and, after the fall of Greece, the Greeks. Only the Australians were not permitted to enter the cities of Egypt. They had wreaked such havoc in the First World War that King Faruk refused to have them. An exception was made for the Australian cricket team who visited once from Palestine. And of course they fought bravely in the Egyptian desert.

And what did the Egyptians make of this invasion? It brought them prosperity. The rich got richer and the small businessmen, the street vendors, the taxi drivers, all profited financially. They also exploited the servicemen, cheating them and over-charging in a country where bargaining was the norm. Anti-British feelings were strong, but in their own interests they kept them suppressed. Egyptian politicians and intellectuals, on the other hand, were split openly into pro-

British and anti-British camps. Servicemen were warned not to go into the poorer districts of Cairo, never to go anywhere alone, even in a taxi. I once saw from the safety of a tram, a soldier being led into the back streets of Bulaq by two Arabs and felt he might never be seen again. I could travel alone in taxis and *gharries* in complete safety and regularly did. I was recognised in some subtle way as a fellow-Cairene.

I remember once taking a *gharrie* home and being over-charged by the driver. I gave him the normal fare, saying in Arabic '*I'm* not an English soldier.' He burst into delighted laughter and drove away still shaking with mirth.

The Egyptian sense of humour – wonderful! If you could make an Egyptian laugh – and it was easy – he was your friend for life.

For their part, the Egyptians needed their sense of humour. One of the most humiliating and painful episodes I ever witnessed was on a Cairo tram. I was sitting in the First Class compartment opposite an Egyptian gentleman. Grey-haired with a fine ascetic face, he was immaculately dressed (Savile Row?), sported a pearl tiepin and held a silver-topped cane. From his appearance one would guess an aristocrat, an intellectual (Senator? High Court judge? – we were near the Law Courts – Courtier?) Two young South African privates jumped on to the platform outside and one of them started to torment the Egyptian. 'Boy, there's a fine tiepin! And where did you get that cane, Boy?' – twiddling the top of the cane. I shrank with embarrassment. The Egyptian coloured slightly, kept his eyes down in dignified silence and clutched his cane more tightly.

The outskirts of Cairo were becoming ringed by camps and the servicemen and women poured into Cairo seeking entertainment on their time off. It was important that it should be found for all these healthy young people.

Officers were well catered for. The Gezira Sporting Club had ready-made sports facilities and to the Saturday night dinner dance at the club was added the Lonely Hearts dance every Tuesday for officers and members of the nursing services. This was initiated by Lady Wavell, wife of General Wavell, Commander-in-Chief of the Middle East Forces, and the Wavells were often to be seen with their daughter, entertaining a party of young men. Many of us civilian girls, sometimes chaperoned, sometimes with partners, went along also.

The big hotels continued to provide dancing and cabarets, but both the best hotels and the Gezira Sporting Club were out of bounds to other ranks. Later in the war, one of the polo fields at the club, not used now most men were fighting or on short Cairo leave, was opened to other ranks. A military band played there and – surprise, surprise – the nannies abandoned the children's playground and took their charges to the polo field, discreetly near the swimming pool but within sight of the soldiers!

More had to be done for the other ranks, who could only otherwise find their entertainment among the cafés, the cinemas and nightclubs of Cairo. Lady Russell, wife of Thomas Russell Pasha, Chief of Police, opened the Victory Club in the centre of Cairo. I never went there, but understand it was mainly a meting place where the men could socialize, eat and get a shower – very important when one lived under canvas in the desert. Lady Russell was usually there herself and middle class English ladies rushed to help. (I used to suspect it was so that later they could say to their friends 'As *Lady Russell* said to me . . .') Some of the other ranks ungratefully referred to her as Lady Vinegar.

Lady Russell also had the imagination to found Music for All, a most remarkable little club off Sharia Kasr el Nil. Grouped round a central reasonably-sized concert hall there were rest rooms, a restaurant and more showers. There were daily gramophone recitals of classical music, daily bridge and chess, regular talks and debates and regular live concerts. One notorious debate towards the end of the war, which alarmed the authorities, took the form of a mock general election. With a resounding majority, the Socialist Party was voted in. Music for All was an oasis of peace and civilisation and, most important of all, it was open to both officers and men. I was to spend many happy hours there, including singing in concerts.

Live classical music was provided for the most part by the amateur Cairo Symphony Orchestra, which did include a few professionals. Then there was the Cairo Area Military Band. The Ladies and Services Choral Society, of which I was a member, used the latter in its concerts, stiffened by strings from the amateur orchestra. A major event was a visit from the Palestine Orchestra, which was composed of refugee Jews from Europe and played to a very high standard.

Live theatre was at first provided by the Cairo Amateur Dramatic Society which had flourished for many years and by visiting – not very good – ENSA parties. Later we were visited by West End companies and among others I remember Adrienne Corri and Emlyn Williams coming out to give us *Blithe Spirit, Flare Path* and *Night Must Fall.* Celebrities also paid us visits – Noel Coward, Larry Adler, Seymour Hicks, Gracie Fields and Jack Benny, to name a few. A small amateur company was started in about 1942 called The New Vic. It consisted mainly of professional actors who found themselves in uniform in Cairo and they put on more avant-garde productions.

For those servicemen who were interested there were weekly tours round the mosques and streets of Old Cairo, conducted by a remarkable Frenchwoman, Mrs. Devonshire, an expert in Islamic architecture. My father tried to interest me in these but I stubbornly refused to go along, to my now regret.

Another oasis and source of intellectual stimulus for those in the know was the Anglo-Egyptian Union. Situated almost opposite our flat, it was a club run by the British Council for the promotion of Anglo-Egyptian relations. The grounds were small but peaceful and we regularly went across in the afternoons or evenings to relax on the lawns. It had a well-stocked library, which I used often, and held social and cultural events. It attracted the intelligentsia of Cairo, members of the Council or the P.I. among others. Robin Fedden, Terence Tiller, Keith Bullen, G.S. Fraser, writers and poets all, gathered there. The Union would put on both Egyptian and English plays and concerts. It was there I saw Seymour Hicks and also a hilarious Egyptian film about the housewives of Cairo rebelling and expressing their anger by chasing their husbands over the rooftops of Cairo wielding rolling pins. It was there that I first heard a recital by a male voice choir, the Services Choral Society, conducted by Clifford Harker. Socialising afterwards with the singers, my friend Sheila Jamison and I learned they were hoping to develop it into a mixed voice choir and decided to join.

(The Anglo-Egyptian Union shared its grounds with the Egyptian Officers' Club. I read recently in Anwar el Sadat's autobiography that while we were smugly socialising with the Egyptians at the Union, Sadat was meeting regularly at the Officers' Club with Nahas and Neguib, planning the revolution to get rid of the monarchy and the British.)

The good English ladies of Cairo vied with each other to entertain the soldiers. Our next-door neighbour, Mrs. Bramble, regularly held lunch or evening parties for them and I was often invited to join them. Then, her daughter Daphne, a couple of years younger than me, would invite me to join her to go out with a group of these young men to the cinema or dancing. Sheila Jamison's parents were Methodists and they held open house every Sunday after church to members of the congregation. I went along to one of these gatherings once or twice. The table would be laden with sandwiches and cakes and great pots of tea and we would sing hymns around the upright piano.

Then there were the dances. Every night there was dancing and my memory (inaccurate) tells me I danced my way through the war. One danced at the Club of course and at all the big hotels: Shepheards, where one danced in the gardens in the summer, the Continental roof garden, Mena House by the swimming pool, and the Semiramis until it was commandeered to house GHQ Middle East. There was dancing also at the nightclubs: Jules, the Kursaal, the Kit Kat and many smaller and seedier establishments. One could usually see a poor cabaret at the hotels and clubs, but often we would be provided with an eye-popping Apache dance or belly dance.

Something had to be done to provide opportunities for dancing for the troops. The first troops' dances were held at the Ezbekieh Gardens. They were extraordinary and, in retrospect, quite hilarious.

An announcement would appear in *The Sphinx:* 'A dance for Other Ranks will take place at the Ezbekieh Gardens next Saturday. Ladies of the British Community will be in attendance.' Dutifully, together with other "Ladies of the British Community", I would go along in full evening dress to the flat of a Brigadier and his wife's near the Club. We would be offered a magnificent buffet, after which we would be transported, heavily chaperoned by Army officers' wives, to the Ezbekieh Gardens, which were near Shepheards and the *Muski* and not far from the red light district. I remember a large barn-like building, a live dance band and small tables round the floor at which sat the soldiers, some with women of the town. Having titivated in the cloakroom, we moved en masse to one corner of the room, where we were roped off. By degrees the men would gather before us, examining us critically. We might have been cattle at a sale! When the music started, the rope was dropped, the men rushed and snatched whichever girl they could! When the music ended we retired to our corner and the rope was replaced. Nevertheless, they were great fun, those dances. We were soon to learn that other ranks were better dancers than officers. They had no inhibitions and whirled one round the dance floor, whereas officers tended to shuffle one round awkwardly, making polite conversation.

As far as I know the Ezbekieh dances didn't last long. The churches took up the challenge and offered a dance once a week. By far the wildest troops' dances were in the crypt of St. Joseph's Catholic Cathedral. (During the day the crypt was used as a social centre for the men. It was run by two attractive but dour young girls sent out specially from London by the Catholic Women's League. Later in the war I would serve once a week in the canteen.)

Slightly less wild were the dances at the Anglican Cathedral Hall, but the dances that my friends Sheila and Hazel Jamison and I opted for were at the Church of Scotland in Bulaq. They were smaller, almost family, affairs and the evening always ended with Scottish dancing which we loved. Sheila was the only one of my friends to own a car and we would bowl along in her tiny Baby Austin through the streets of Bulaq to the church hall every Friday.

We were invited to dance everywhere. English girls were few and much in demand. I danced at all the hotels, at the club, at private houses, at nightclubs. Sometimes we would taxi out to the Pyramids Road to dance at the Auberge des Pyramides, the most glamorous and beautifully designed open-air nightclub. There were two dance floors, one raised, and they were divided by fountains. Sometimes I felt we could have been dancing on an Astaire-Rogers film set. I only have two snapshot memories of the Auberge: a bomber pilot musing on how extraordinary it was that only a few days before he had been dropping bombs on people, and now was dancing under a star-studded sky – and an ugly quarrel between some Afrikaners and some South African soldiers of English origin.

There was the Carlton, also on the Pyramids Road, which was much cheaper and basic. I remember a wooden building with a dance floor in the centre, ringed by a verandah where one ate extremely good food. Dancing was to a wind-up gramophone. It was at the Carlton that I was as near to death as I was ever to be during the war (there were two other occasions). As we sat at our meal, looking out over the flat fields to the desert, a low-flying plane came past, almost at the same level as us. 'Oh look!' I cried. 'Look at those pretty red lights!' The next moment Daphne and I had been pulled under the table by our South African escorts. The pretty red lights had been tracer bullets and the plane a German one, for some reason cruising near Cairo and miles from the front.

We were often invited to dance at camps out in the desert, climbing into the backs of lorries for the journey there. A dance floor would have been erected under canvas. Once we went to a South African military hospital and during the evening Daphne Bramble and I visited a ward. The men lay on low beds, again under canvas. We must have looked like angels from Heaven to them, or at the very least starlets from Hollywood, with our long colourful evening dresses and long shining hair.

For my evening dresses – and indeed all my dresses – I went to Rosie, a little Moroccan Jewish girl. She lived in a mansion flat off Sharia Soliman Pasha with a large extended family. In one of the bedrooms I would see a very old woman plumped up on pillows in a high bed. At the far end of the flat there was a large room with a long table at which several young girls sat, sewing, machining and chattering. The fitting room was a cell-like room with a small window high up in the wall. An unframed long mirror leaned against the wall and the floor was piled high with film magazines. I would bring in my material and Rosie would rummage among the magazines, then show me an exquisite creation worn by Joan Crawford or Jeannette MacDonald and say 'That's the one for you.' And she was always right and for 25 piastres (25p) I would have a gorgeous new dress. Those were the days of nipped-in waists and flowing skirts in Hollywood and as there was no clothes rationing in Egypt we could indulge ourselves. I had two evening dresses at any one time, most memorably one of shimmering blue and silver Muski brocade, until it was rivalled by a champagne-coloured floating affair that I had worn as a bridesmaid.

I didn't "dance my way through the war." Of course it wasn't quite like that, although there can't have been many weeks when I didn't dance at least once.

I was only sixteen when the war broke out and under certain restrictions. I was not allowed to go out alone with a young man until I was eighteen, although to go in a foursome was permissible. I remember asking my father's permission to use face powder on my eighteenth birthday. Before that I would comb my eyebrows, pinch my cheeks and bite my lips before walking into a party, tricks taught me by the Vernon Jarvis sisters.

Also Joan's illness placed severe limits on what I could do. When there was no living-in carer I only went out occasionally. I would settle Joan down for the night and leave her alone until my father returned from the Turf Club. I've wondered since what her feelings were, being left and unable to move from her bed.

I wasn't alone in being limited. Daphne Bramble, next door, had a very strict father who decreed she could only go out once a week and she and her mother occasionally tried to outwit him. On one occasion Uncle Don invited us both to join a party at the club dinner dance as Donald was in Cairo on leave. We went down in the lift, in our long dresses and accompanied by young RAF officers, to be met at the bottom by Mr. Bramble. 'Oh dear!' said Daphne and drew him aside to give him an explanation. When she re-joined us she said that she and her mother had put a bolster in her bed to deceive her father into thinking that she was asleep! She was hoping against hope that he wouldn't find out.

Once Joan was better and I was nearly twenty, I have to confess I had a Very Good Time – dances, dinners, theatre, concerts and singing – although I was also still given to periods of depression and discontent.

So, it was both good and bad. It took a long while for Joan and me to become on friendly terms, not helped by my aloofness and by her jealousy. There was the astonishing occasion when she burnt all the letters I had written from Cambridge and which my father had given me to read. I never got to read them all. And the other occasion when she gave my childhood teddy bear to the little girl upstairs without consulting me. But we did eventually come to terms and were drawn together by her illness.

There were times that I felt guilty that life was so easy materially for us when London was being bombed nightly and I decided that our family's "cross" (a Catholic concept) was Joan's illness – which, after all, was the direct result of the war.

The war dominated our lives and we followed the news greedily and I found myself rejoicing at every German plane shot down over England. We got used to the regular news of yet another friend killed or wounded or taken prisoner. Sometimes I think we formed protective emotional shields against feeling too much.

One of the greatest pleasures during those years was singing in a choir, as it was to be for most of my adult life.

Sheila Jamison and I joined Clifford Harker's choir when he transformed it from a male voice choir to a mixed voice one. Clifford had been an organist and choirmaster in the North of England and had formed a male voice choir on the troop-ship coming out to the Middle East. It would have been a long journey, round the Cape of Good Hope, as the Mediterranean was closed to all but warships. He had made such a reputation for himself by the time he reached Egypt that he was seconded to form a choir in Cairo and to be the Artistic Director of Music for All.

He started off the mixed choir modestly with sacred music and folk music, but soon progressed to the *Messiah,* Haydn's *Seasons* and Brahms' *Requiem.* There were no auditions and the men outnumbered the women by two to one. The men came and went as their tours of duty in Cairo ended. It was interesting to note that it seemed that most of the men came from the North of England, not Wales as one might have imagined. Clifford was a good-natured conductor and got good results from this not very promising material.

We rehearsed in the Anglican Cathedral hall and gave most concerts in the cathedral itself, although our concerts of light music – Gilbert and Sullivan, *Merrie England,* etc. – took place at Music for All.

Sheila and I particularly befriended three of the young men, all from Yorkshire. We would often go off after rehearsal to an inappropriately named café, The Big Ben, for a drink and gossip. My father, all through the war, would wait up for me until I came home from an evening out, often tarnishing the memory of a good time, of course! One night I got home at midnight, two hours after rehearsal had ended.

'Where on earth have you been?'

'Discussing the Beveridge Report.'

My father grunted. In fact we, and the men particularly, had been most impressed and excited by the Report, which laid the foundations for the post-war Welfare State.

Our most memorable concert was the *Messiah* in October 1942. We were in the middle of what was known at the time as "The Flap". ("To flap" was an RAF stiff-upper-lip term meaning "to panic".) Rommel and his troops had got as far as El Alamein, within sixty miles of Alexandria, and had halted there. We were much later to learn that this was partly because Rommel had run out of supplies and partly because the German tanks had been unable to negotiate the Qattara Depression, a particularly hostile valley in the desert. But at the time his presence so near to us was threatening.

There followed "The Flap". First to leave the country was the Royal Navy which steamed out of Alexandria harbour. This may have been tactically necessary, but it was *not* good for morale . . . My father was taken on to a roof-top in Garden City to watch the British Embassy burning all its papers in the garden . . . British officers were unable to retrieve their uniforms from the laundry because the latter openly hoped to sell them to the Germans when they arrived . . . Civilians fled. Friends left for South Africa. Civilian employees of British government offices were put into uniform so that they could be moved quickly to Palestine. (This would have been an option for me but again it felt like treachery to leave my parents behind. I reconciled myself to the prospect of being interned and promised myself I would write "that novel".)

The RAF and Army stood fast, ready for any development and the streets still swarmed with servicemen.

The choir were due to give a performance of the *Messiah* and so we did. The Cathedral was packed. In the seats of honour sat the British Ambassador and the Bishop of Egypt and the Sudan. For the rest it was a sea of uniforms. The audience crowded the side aisles, sat in the window embrasures and dome, packed themselves in behind the choir and pressed themselves against the doors and windows outside. The performance was also broadcast by the BBC: 'The Huns may have invaded Egypt but the *Messiah* goes on.' It was a highly emotional evening.

Some random memories . . .

. . . Walking home after a night out in Cairo, which I liked to do. The astonishing Egyptian moonlight, like a cascade of silver illuminating everything as bright as in day. The sky studded with stars, the Nile shining in the night light.

. . . And how have I got this far without mentioning two of the most notable features of Egypt, the palm trees and the flies? Palm trees grew everywhere, in roads, in gardens, gracefully rising above us. On the outskirts of Cairo one could sometimes see Arabs picking the dates. They tied a sling around their buttocks and round the serrated trunk of the tree. Then, barefooted, they would work their way up to the fruit which they would put in a soft basket slung round the waist.

. . . As for the flies, there were so *many* of them and they were *everywhere*. Unlike their more good-natured English counterparts, they would swoop and dive-bomb around the room. Then one would land on a nearby table, vigorously rubbing its front feet together before attacking and landing on one's face or bare arm. I don't know why so few English people sported the fly whisks the Egyptians had: thick brushes of (?) animal hair with ornate, decorated handles.

. . . Driving out into the desert for the pleasure of it. It was said that the south-eastern area round the Pyramids was mined and it was certainly out of bounds. To the west of Mena House and near the desert road, camps sprang up. One always knew when one was passing an Indian regiment because the tents had miniature gardens flourishing in the sand just outside.

. . . My twenty-first birthday party for which Joan was now well enough to act hostess. All the strands of my life were drawn together: old family friends from early childhood, the group of young officer friends currently in Cairo, girlfriends, and my MOI colleagues.

. . . Spending a lazy afternoon with a young officer whose name and face I now forget. We sat in chaises longues on the edge of the cricket pitch, lazily watching the game, taking tea and talking. We discussed P.G. Wodehouse and Noel Coward. The latter had recently been touring the camps and had been an overwhelming success. It was an altogether delightful afternoon and when I heard a fortnight later that my companion had been killed in action I was glad for him that we had had it.

Performance of Messiah during "The Flap."
All Saints Cathedral, Cairo. September 1942.

Dinner at Shepheards. Left to Right: Charles Mackintosh, Nancy Orr, Major Mackay, my father, myself.

My father receiving the Order of the Nile
from King Farouk. 1945

Donald, Spitfire pilot.

With my step-mother
1944

Reception at Anglo-Egyptian Union.
Egyptian Officers' Club in background.

Gary Cooper and Greek actress reading AEPA.

Mollie Clark. Riverwood, 1945

Family and Friends

Everybody's life was changed by the war. Our small family suffered as an indirect consequence of it. Joan's illness was precipitated by the impossibility of getting proper treatment for her TB, my father's business nearly went to the wall.

My father must have been under the most enormous strain all through those war years. There was the constant worry and cost of his wife's illness; he had to face the possibility of closing down *The Sphinx* and did in the end have to sell it, and I must have been great cause for anxiety. We had lost our earlier intimacy and although I lived and worked with him, in a subtle way I was beyond his control and influence. If I had led a conventional young girl's life shared between club and home, things might have been different. As it was, my casual club life with my peers ended when I got a job long before they did. I deliberately rejected their way of life, chose my friends where I would and roamed the streets of Cairo freely. It wasn't as delinquent as that sounds, but it was wayward and my father was an Edwardian father at heart and had social ambitions for me.

He also had to compete with the best journalists Fleet Street could send out, although his brief was slightly different: to concentrate on Egyptian affairs. On the other hand his more prestigious colleagues were always most friendly and it has struck me since that they were an extremely relaxed, mutually co-operative bunch. They shared and discussed the news and political situation generously and openly, although they were of course in competition with one another.

My father stood up to these stresses remarkably well. He was over sixty when the war broke out, but he only ever had minor illnesses: a day's lumbago or "gippy tummy". At the time of the takeover of *The Sphinx* by the SOP he lost the ability to sign his cheques and had to devise a new signature for the bank. That was the most obvious outward sign of stress he ever showed. In spite of his frantic lifestyle and apart from a new brusqueness, he remained calm and self-contained.

Joan bore her illness stoically and patiently. It was only when she was recovering that she became irritable and demanding from time to time. By that stage we were getting on well enough and to my surprise I discovered that she could be thoughtful and kind when I was unwell or in trouble.

In England my mother remained in London throughout, surviving the Blitz and then the doodlebugs. Ardisheer had died and at first she lived alone, but soon shared a flat with a friend called Nina, whom I never met. By the end of the war she had become a confirmed and serious alcoholic.

Aunt Rosie evacuated with Jane to Glastonbury, where they stayed until the war was nearly over. Jane was still at school and was showing signs of being extremely bright.

Peggy joined up in the ATS and was soon manning an anti-aircraft battery on Blackheath. Later she was to serve in Belgium after the Allies had invaded France and she was to win the MBE for her welfare work with her girls. Towards the end of the war she married Leif Rovick, an American GI.

Donald joined up in the RAF as soon as he was eighteen and went to train in Canada, where he was later to emigrate. He wasn't in the famous Battle of Britain, but he was in the almost equally terrible bombing of Malta. (The average life expectancy of Spitfire pilots at that time was one month. Pause for a moment and reflect on the implications of that.) Then he was moved to Egypt, where he fought in the Western Desert. He was awarded the Distinguished Flying Cross for bravery in the field. He would come on leave to Cairo from time to time and we always met. Uncle Don was also in Cairo all through the war and was said to be involved in secret war work – although I'm not sure if that was just a rumour or not. (Donald had his twenty-first birthday in Cairo and Joan decided we should give him a brandy flask 'in case he needs some to steady his nerves when he's in the air.' Donald dissolved into laughter when I told him this. Brandy was the last thing he needed when every nerve had to be concentrated on the battle! But Joan always took a flask of medicinal brandy when she travelled. It was an accepted antidote in those days for "nerves" or "gippy tummy", laced with ginger ale for the latter.)

Aunt Vi was the member of the family who was probably to suffer the most as the result of the war. Of her three sons, she was to lose two. Eddy – handsome, debonair Eddy who had been ASM at the Abbey Theatre, Dublin, with aspirations to go on the stage – joined the Navy. He rose to be Naval Attaché in India and was married when he disappeared. 'Missing, believed killed' would have been the official Admiralty message, and Aunt Vi was never to learn how he had disappeared. Her second son, Frank, fought as a rear gunner in the RAF and was so shattered by his experiences in the war that he found it difficult to keep a job afterwards. He was living with Aunt Vi when he went out one day, hired a room in a small hotel and gassed himself. John, the youngest, remained to her. He hadn't joined up because he was a conscientious objector – and in any case an Irishman, so not subject to conscription. His brothers volunteered to serve, as did many Southern Irishmen in both World Wars. Aunt Rosie had been engaged to one of them who was killed in the Great War before she met Uncle Don.

Mollie and John Clark's house in Kent received a direct hit but they all survived and moved to Cookham Dean in Berkshire. John's family had owned since Victorian times two boathouses on the Thames and they went to live there. They introduced electricity and built a bathroom with an Elsanol loo. One boathouse was used as bedrooms and the other had a living-room and kitchen. John continued to work for the family firm refining sugar for breweries but this had moved from the dangerous area of London's Isle of Dogs to Manchester. He would commute home for weekends.

One day, my father drew me aside to tell me that Jeannine and Romalita, Mollie's daughters, were missing, probably killed. In due course Philip O'Farrell (of the London Letter) wrote to give us the details.

Mollie's first husband had taken the children to Cornwall for a holiday with his second wife and mother-in-law. One day he had chartered a plane to take them all from St. Ives to the Scilly Isles for the day. When they were due to return either a German air raid along the South coast had started or the weather was poor, and the pilot had protested it was too dangerous to fly back to the mainland. John Leggitt had insisted: 'I hired you. You do what I say'; but the plane never reached St. Ives. For some weeks nobody knew what had happened until one day some wreckage and clothing was washed ashore.

Mollie had an uncanny gift, if you can call it that, of foretelling disaster or death. After the plane went missing I received a letter from her written beforehand saying that she had secretly gone to stay in a hotel in Cornwall because 'I feel sure something is going to happen to the girls. I don't know what and they don't know I'm here.' A few days later she was sitting in the hotel foyer when she heard first reports of the plane's disappearance. John and his second wife were well-known media people so the news was widely reported. I don't think Mollie ever really recovered from this tragedy.

Mollie's brother Gerry was called up at the outbreak of the war and was taken prisoner at the fall of Dunkirk. He spent the war years in prisoner of war camps in Germany and

Poland. We corresponded sporadically. We were only allowed to send twenty-five words on special official cards and no photographs. After the war he was to tell me a poignant story. When his pre-war girlfriend wrote in 1944 to tell him that she had become engaged to someone else, his name went up on the camp's "Roll of Honour" which listed the names of prisoners whose wives or sweethearts had left them for another man. Having survived the war, he was tragically drowned in the Thames near Mollie's home in the mid-Forties. He never knew his son, who is now a GP in Surrey.

Of my school friends I heard regularly from Mary Reynolds, who joined the WAAF and was engaged to a music producer at the BBC. She died suddenly of a brain haemorrhage – news brought to me by her cousin Ernest who was serving in the Middle East. Cecily Randall had a high-powered job with the Ministry of Information and Bee went first to Cheltenham Ladies College to finish her schooling, and then up to Cambridge.

My two best girlfriends during the war were Sheila Jamison and Elizabeth Thomson.

Sheila and I became close friends as a result of singing in the choir together and going to the Scots Church dances. She worked on top-secret work in the Censorship's laboratory, her sister at HQ, British Troops in Egypt. They were Northern Irish and their father was in the Egyptian State Railways. They lived in an attractive flat nearby on two floors. A real novelty to go upstairs to bed! Most of our friends lived in flats, though a few lived in villas. I remember tea on the lawn in the English fashion with some friends in Ma'adi, a Cairo suburb. Even the wealthiest Cairenes lived in modest villas compared to the huge piles their counterparts would have built in England. Presumably this was due to the severe shortage of building land in the Nile Delta.

Elizabeth Thomson I had known before on summer holidays in Egypt. Her father was manager of Barclays Bank. Like me she was a slightly gauche girl straight out of a convent school. Our parents both decided we were good company for one another and we did indeed get on instinctively. Like me at first she wasn't allowed out alone with a young man and we often made up a foursome to go out for the evening. She was a pretty blonde with a delightful sense of humour and her one great regret was that she couldn't fall in love. (She made good this deficiency after the war.) As I had been in and out of love all my life I found this very difficult to understand. When Rommel got to Alamein giving rise to "The Flap", she and her mother went to South Africa, returning again in 1943.

Liz and Sheila represented two different aspects of my life. Sheila was choir and the Scots Church. Elizabeth, the club and young officers and discreet dinners.

The third steady friendship I made during the war was with Major Mackay. He had worked in Cairo in the Twenties and was a friend of my father's. But after the death in infancy of their only child he and his wife had returned to England where he worked in Manchester. When I knew him he must have been in his forties. He took an avuncular interest in me. I was quite unable to talk to my father about things close to my heart, but I could and did confide in Major Mackay. He was never "heavy" in handling these confidences and helped me to keep a sense of humour. He was a good dear friend and I owed a lot to his counsel. He often invited me to tea or for a drink and I was included in all his parties. My first holiday of the war was spent in Luxor at the Winter Palace Hotel with him and his friend, Mollie Grimes. She was another protégée of his, a vivacious redhead in her thirties. I may be naïve, but I believed their relationship was entirely honourable; Major Mackay was the perfect old-fashioned gentleman. Mollie, like a whole group of English people in Cairo at that time, was a refugee from German-occupied Greece, where she had been teaching. I knew her well because she sang in the choir. We had a wonderful fortnight in Upper Egypt and Major Mackay looked after us both well. Mollie was to marry a wealthy Greek widower whom she had met in Cairo and acquired two stepdaughters.

These were my deep friendships, but there were many, many other people who drifted in and out of my life in a way that was only possible in war-time, as people passed through Cairo or were stationed there for a short while. One always recognised that time was short and friendships blossomed quickly and sometimes briefly. Often, after they had left Cairo, one didn't hear from friends again. They were mostly men friends. English girls were scarce in Cairo.

And some encounters were more bizarre than others. Here are some, in no particular order . . .

. . . Wally! One day leaving *The Sphinx* offices I was approached by a young private. He wanted to buy some gloves for his girl-friend in England and was sure my hands were the same size. Would I help him buy some? What a chat-up line! Because one was automatically friendly towards servicemen at that time, I agreed to buy gloves with him. A few weeks later he was waiting for me again. The gloves had fitted her a treat. Would I now help him to buy something else, I don't remember exactly what? So off we went and did the shopping. After that he would often be hovering on the corner as I came out of the office and we would go off and have a coffee, or even maybe a lunch. I think we can only have talked nostalgically of England.

. . . The two Leslies. Leslie B. was a member of ENSA in a clerical capacity, a small, plump young man who had been a piano tuner before the war, presumably because he was one of the generation for whom there was no money for further

177

education. He was in fact extremely knowledgeable about music with a particular love of organ music. He became the music critic for *The Sphinx* and often took me to concerts on the press tickets. We also maintained an almost constant telephonic communication because he was invariably late with his copy. He was a fierce critic, making no allowances for the difficulties under which music was made in wartime Egypt. ... I also got to know his friend Leslie W., who was a church organist in Durham, older than us, gentle and a perfect contrast to Leslie B's acerbic wit. He worked with Peter Haddon (former actor, later to own Wimbledon Theatre) who was responsible for the broadcast of Family Favourites to the Middle East. Each week they would visit a different camp and interview men who chose their music and recorded messages to their families. The recordings would then be sent to the BBC in London. A long-winded way of doing it, but the only way available at the time. Their secretary offered me her job when she went home to England on health grounds, but I was dug in at the MOI and didn't accept it.

... Daphne Bramble, my next-door neighbour and two years younger than me. When war broke out she was still at the English School (which had moved from Bulaq to the more salubrious suburb of Heliopolis). Haile Selassie, Emperor of Ethiopia, and his family, exiled from their homeland temporarily, took refuge in Cairo. The small princesses went to the English School and Daphne took a protective interest in them. One would see them now and again going into the flat to spend the afternoon with her. As soon as she was old enough Daphne started the round of parties and dances and I was usually included. She was petite, like a piece of Dresden china, pretty and impishly flirtatious. She was always getting into scrapes of her own making. It was typical of her that one day I heard her calling me from her bathroom window which faced our hall window over the building's well. She had promised to go out with three different men that evening and now they were all turning up at the front door for her mother to deal with while she hid in the bathroom.

. . . John Spedding, who spent his week's leave helping me bring out *The Sphinx* so that my father could have his first few days' holiday of the war. He was a sergeant who had been a journalist in New Zealand and now worked on the NZ paper for the forces in the Middle East. He must have been in his thirties, had a dry wit and tried to arouse my interest in politics. He gave me, for instance, a copy of Ignazio Silone's *Fontamara,* a Communist writer's account of the poverty-stricken conditions of an Italian mountain village. But I was too self-absorbed in those years to develop a social conscience – that was to come much later – but it's interesting that I do remember being affected by the book. John and I became close friends and had some good times together. He went with his paper to Bari in Italy once the Allies had invaded that country and wrote to me for a short while.

. . . Elsie and Vivian Vernon Jarvis. Although I only rarely visited the club after I got a job, I kept in touch with the two sisters. They took me under their wing when I first arrived from boarding school, invited me to their parties (one memorable one we went on a scavenging hunt in cars. The hardest thing to find was a camel's hair. Eventually we found an Arab who was prepared to cut one off for us, but we didn't win). Vivian married a doctor serving at one of the military hospitals and had a baby, William, while still very young. I envied her.

. . . Bill, a cheeky New Zealander who claimed to have been the youngest soldier in the NZ Army. He had lied about his age and joined up at the age of sixteen. I can't remember where we acquired him (probably a Bramble party for the troops), but he would turn up on the doorstep with his battledress tunic bulging with NAAFI tea and sugar and coffee, all rationed to civilians.

. . . Derek, another serviceman who adopted us. He was a church organist and I suspect was attracted by my grand piano as much as he was by the open fire and tea awaiting him. One day he presented me with a puppy, an adorable ball of white fluff. But he was a *pye* dog, a wild desert dog. Some street vendors had hit on the idea of selling the puppies to the gullible and sentimental soldiery, but they would all grow into quite ugly dogs. I adored my puppy whom I christened George and for a while kept him in the flat. Joan was in hospital so could raise no objections. However, George wasn't house-trained and when Joan came home he was banished to the roof with the *suffragi*. Eventually Frieda, Joan's carer, rescued him and found him a home with a family in Helwan.

. . . Bob, one of three cadets who joined the choir while going through OCTU (Officers' Cadet Training Unit). Bob was older than the other two, one of whom I was to get engaged to. Bob was married and was the wit of the party. I'm not sure I'd find him so funny now, but at the time we thought him hilarious. The witticisms poured from his lips. I remember he and I had been to see *The Road to Morocco* with Bob Hope and Bing Crosby and were in merry mood. Walking home along the Corniche by the Nile he made me laugh so much I became incapable of taking another step (and we hadn't touched alcohol, I promise you). Bob had to hail a *gharrie* to get me home.

. . . Jo Taylor, the cousin I never knew I had. He contacted us from a military hospital outside Cairo where he was recovering from a wound at sea. When he was convalescent he came to see us. Dressed in official convalescent bright "blues" with white shirt and red tie, he sported a fearsome black beard. Only sailors were allowed to grow beards. We clicked instantly, in an almost uncanny way, and talked and laughed and talked for the three days he was in Cairo. When he left to rejoin his ship he sent me what seemed like the contents of a flower shop. My father chuckled in disbelief when he saw me at my desk surrounded by a sea of flowers.

With extraordinary lack of curiosity on my part, I never asked how he fitted into the family.

I never saw or heard from him again.

Then there were all the family friends, most of whom I had known since childhood . . .

. . . Lucienne and Max Fischer, who was my father's business partner. She was an elegant, sharp-witted Parisienne, he was an older, shambling French Jew. I suspect their marriage may not ever have been very good (it was said her first husband had committed suicide after losing money at the gambling tables of Monte Carlo. Maybe she had married on the rebound). It was under incredible strain during the war. Max supported the Free French cause. Lucienne supported the collaborator Marshal Petain, honouring the "my country, right or wrong" principle. We invited André Glarner, a French journalist friend, to meet the Fischers, but the political argument between him and Lucienne became so bitter that she asked him to leave.

. . . André Glarner, who had been Paris correspondent for the *Daily Telegraph* and now found himself in the Middle East. A large, swash-buckling man, he had a strong personality and I was persuaded to type the manuscript of a book he had written about his wartime experiences: *De Montmartre à Tripoli*. I can't think when I found the time to do this, but in due course it was finished. He didn't pay me any money, but promised me instead a length of Damascus brocade, usually beautiful and highly prized. The brocade was going to be delivered in Cairo by Alice Delysia, then a famous music hall artiste. Andy and I went to Shepheard's Hotel to take delivery and were received by Alice Delysia in her room. She was reclining on a large double bed dressed in scarlet silk pyjamas. (It has only now struck me that there might have been any significance in her receiving a gentleman in such attire in the middle of the day!) Her dressing table was smothered in photographs of herself. I thought to myself that this all must be typical of an actress. I sat modestly in the corner while Andy and Alice greeted each other effusively. After a while, she looked at me and said 'But Andy, this brocade would be most unsuitable for so young and pretty a girl!' So I didn't get it. It was beautiful, in a gold cloth embroidered with figures of birds and animals. Andy and I accepted this manipulation gracefully and a few days later he took me to the Muski where he bought a lovely length of blue and silver Egyptian brocade and it made my favourite evening dress.

. . . The Wildmans. Lou Wildman was managing director of Cable and Wireless, a bachelor who had travelled widely with the firm in peacetime. He was sitting in his Cairo office one day during the war when a beautiful young blonde was ushered in. He recognised her as a girl he'd had a brief flirtation with in Latvia.

'What are you doing here?' he asked.

'I've come to marry you' was the reply.

As he said to my father afterwards: 'What else could I do?' She had travelled, alone, from Russian-occupied Latvia, through Russia, Iran, Palestine and Egypt to reach him. So they were married – an incongruous pair, middle-aged, small man, tall slim young blonde – and I like to think they lived happily ever after.

. . . Sidney and Rosa Sayer, to whom I have referred before. Sidney was a large Cockney with a large personality to match. His wife, Swiss, had been a nurse and was active in the Red Cross. They were unbelievably kind to us during Joan's illness, in countless and varied ways. I'm not sure how my father and I would have survived it without their concern and help.

. . . The Titteringtons, the Goldings, the Cartlands, Mr. Craig (who was to be killed in the Cairo riots and who had devoted his life to Egypt as a Civil Servant), Stephen Trimen, the Burrills, the de Termes. The names are endless and stories could be told about all of them. Then they were quite simply our very good friends. In retrospect they seem to have been larger than life, curiously interesting people, for the most part eccentric and opinionated. Perhaps they had to be, to be true Cairenes, to devote their adult life to Egypt, unlike the birds of passage in the services and in business.

Love . . .

You fall in love with whom you meet and I fell in love with Charlie.

Having largely cut myself off from life at the Club when I went to work, it was perhaps inevitable that I should be attracted by my young despatch rider at the Censorship. He was older than me – twenty-three to my seventeen years – and he was no beauty and what we had in common apart from our youth I'm not very sure. My preferred reading at the time was Jane Austen and a Life of Diaghilev. His were comics, which he sat reading in the corridor between his deliveries.

Nothing might have developed between us if Mrs. J-B, in her usual bossy way, hadn't decided to intervene. She must have noticed us eyeing one another and having murmured conversations and she rang up Joan to say that she suspected that we were meeting after work on the way home. We weren't doing anything of the sort and I was able honestly to reassure Joan.

'But,' I thought, 'what a good idea!'

And so we did start to meet briefly in the evenings. Secretly. Apart from the fact that I wasn't allowed out alone with a young man, I knew my father would have been extremely upset if he had known about the affair.

Of course the one thing that gave our relationship its particular zest was the secrecy. And I know now that it was a classic adolescent rebellion on my part. I must have been still angry with my father for marrying Joan and if I had had to choose the one thing to punish him by giving him sleepless nights it would have been to have an affair with an older man, a Cockney from the East End about whom we knew nothing.

Charlie never did talk to me about his family. Perhaps he didn't have one. All I knew about him was that he came from

Poplar, then a deprived area, had joined the Regular Army as a boy soldier and had two passions: his motorbike and jazz.

He had taken part in pre-war Military Tattoos and one had to be particularly skilled and brave to do that on a motorbike. Split-second timing was needed to execute Tattoo manoeuvres and he had also been chosen to be one of the riders who drove through a hoop of flames. I was very impressed by this! As for music, Charlie played the double bass as a freelance in dance bands and was part of a small jazz group that played at the large Cairo hotels and that had been broadcast by the BBC.

Soon we became bolder and began to meet in the long afternoons between lunch and evening work. To start with we met at the Oriental Gardens on the Nile. We also met at the Aquarium Gardens near the flat, until one day we were spotted by one of Joan's bridge-playing friends, a teacher taking her class round the grotto.

So Charlie then would hire a car for the afternoon and we would drive out into the desert or through the fields of the Delta. The experience of driving through the unspoilt Egyptian countryside and villages is one I wouldn't have had if I hadn't known Charlie. It was on one of these trips that I first missed death (or at least injury) by inches. We were sitting in the car outside an Arab village when suddenly Charlie leapt from his seat, drawing his pistol. An Egyptian was approaching us with a drawn knife. As soon as he saw Charlie's gun, he ran away and we drove back to Cairo, fast!

We also met at the troops' dances at the Ezbekieh Gardens and the Scots Church. It was sitting out in the Ezbekieh Gardens (I must have escaped the eagle eyes of our chaperones) that we had a conversation that I've often remembered. Charlie was still a signalman – a private – and had been approached by his Sergeant Major to become a Freemason. He was told there would be no chance of promotion and joining the Sergeants' Mess unless he did so.

Having been warned against Freemasonry by the Catholic Church, I advised him against such a move. These were the early days of the war and no doubt as the death toll in the desert rose, promotion in the forces came naturally according to merit. I was however to remember our conversation years later when I confirmed from my own personal and professional experiences that, rightly or wrongly, it was never a bad career move to become a Mason.

Charlie and I were still sustained by the excitement of the "secret affair", but of course my parents must have known about it. They said nothing, until one night when Joan was in hospital and my father safely, I thought, at the Turf Club, the latter came home early to find I was out with Charlie. When I got home we had the one and only row of our relationship. I felt I had the final word when I accused my father of being a snob and disapproving of Charlie because he was a Cockney.

I had by now become stubborn. In my heart of hearts I was beginning to realise Charlie and I were not suited for a long-term relationship, but I was extremely fond of him and we had some good times together. I couldn't give him up. Pride entered into it, too.

Charlie decided to come into the open. He wrote my father a long letter declaring his honourable intentions and even braved him at *The Sphinx* offices. I don't remember that my father gave any noticeable reaction to this, but suddenly Charlie was posted to the desert for a few months. I wondered if my father had "had a word" with someone in authority as he was wont to do. Most probably not, but the thought crossed my mind. In his absence my father made several attempts to interest me in other more eligible young men, but without success.

When Charlie eventually came back to Cairo I began to realise that my feelings for him had changed but stubbornly continued to see him.

Uncle Don came to the rescue as he so often had done before when our family were in crisis. His first move was to persuade my father to allow us to meet openly. So Charlie and I were allowed to go to the pictures together on Sunday afternoons. Awkward afternoons they turned out to be, too! Then Uncle Don invited us both to a drinks party at his *pension.* The moment we walked in I realised that Charlie and I came from different worlds. He was ill at ease, friendly though the other guests were. Uncle Don took us out to the Kursaal, a nightclub and in return was invited to a dance on a houseboat at which Charlie was playing in the band. After this party, Uncle said 'I don't believe you are the least bit in love with Charlie.' And of course by then he was right and those evenings spelt the beginning of the end of the affair.

(In 1947, travelling on the Tube to go and visit Lena and Ian in North London, I saw an unshaven sergeant sitting opposite me. I recognised the scar on his cheek and the inevitable comic that he was reading. It was Charlie, now promoted and returning home from night duty at Knightsbridge Barracks. He joined me and we picked up as though the years hadn't intervened. We got off the train together and talked and talked in the street. It was lovely to see him again. He was now married to a Maltese girl who had sung with his dance band and was the proud father of a small boy. We exchanged phone numbers but never in fact used them.)

I am going to mention two other romances, partly because they were significant to me and partly because they illustrate the difficulties of falling in love in wartime.

Fred was a South African, one of a large group whom I had met at the Brambles and with whom Daphne and I went out a great deal. He was a handsome, gentle young man, reserved at first, but we were drawn to one another and soon became a twosome.

One evening four of us were in a taxi going to the pictures. Jimmy was talking to Daphne and I wasn't listening to him until I heard him say 'Of course it's different for men like Fred who are married.' I sat in shocked silence, wondering if I'd heard correctly. I was still a good-enough Catholic girl with a certain code of behaviour and married men were strictly out of bounds. But we were too involved by then. In the interval at the cinema – it was *Hellzapoppin* I remember – a soldier came up to Fred. 'Hi Fred! How are you? And how's the wife and kid?' So it was true. When I later tackled him about it, Fred said he was sure I had known. He had been quite open about his marriage and had shown photographs around at a party at Music for All. He was sure I must have known.

We continued to meet and his reserve was suddenly broken down. He was in fact extremely unhappy about his marriage, because he believed his wife was having an affair with another man. We would have long, long telephone conversations and otherwise met to go out with the usual gang.

In due course, Fred was posted to the desert, where he saw action, and when he returned to Cairo on leave he had aged to a shocking degree. His hair was starting to go grey and his face was a fine network of lines. Whether this was due to service in the desert or whether it was due to anxiety about his marriage it was hard to know. Probably a bit of both.

He showed me a letter from his wife confessing to having an affair and asking for a divorce. What seemed to hurt Fred as much as anything was that the other man was a member of the Bruderbond, a South African Nazi organisation and a powerful force behind the Apartheid movement. She was being unfaithful to him with such a man when he was risking his life in a war against Fascism.

We didn't meet again after that Cairo leave, but kept in touch. After the war he wrote to say he had happily married again: 'She reminds me of you.' That was nice of him! I was very, very fond of Fred.

I was twenty when I had the first really deep relationship with a man. I nearly added the adjective "mature", but in fact I was still very young and unstable. I often felt at odds with the world and one of the qualities I remember about Desmond was his ability to calm me down and lighten my mood. The other thing I remember vividly is how greedily we talked: there was never enough time to say all we had to say.

I had noticed Desmond as a friend of Clifford Harker's. He sang bass in the choir, was stationed at GHQ and helped Clifford with the administrative work entailed in running rehearsals and putting on concerts. Then he was posted to the desert and fought as a gunner at the Battle of el Alamein. When he returned to Cairo and the choir it was to go through OCTU (Officers' Cadet Training Corps). He came from Crosby, a suburb of Liverpool and had been to Merchant Taylor's. His father had been a captain with the Cunard Line and he had a married sister.

We first got to know each other at a choir dance and soon were going out together. Our romance seemed to me at the time to be perfect. I was in love for the first time certainly and surely. And Desmond was a delightful companion. A slender young man of twenty-three with large expressive eyes and a quick Irish wit inherited from his mother. He was also understanding and caring and had an impressive inner strength for one so young. We talked of marriage, but, the future being so uncertain, decided to wait.

When his OCTU course was ended he was again posted to the desert. I felt devastated, bereft. We wrote almost daily and in due course he proposed and I accepted.

I decided to wait until I was twenty-one before telling my parents. I felt my father would not approve, although Joan would have been pleased because she liked Desmond. I also wanted to be legally free to marry whom I liked. When I did tell my father he said 'A very nice young man, but you hardly know anything about him.' I was indignant. I had known him three months and that was a *long time*. As indeed it was in wartime.

So, we got engaged and I began to plan my return to England in order to marry Desmond.

He was by now in the UK, preparing for the invasion of Normandy, having fought in the final battles that pushed Rommel and the Germans west across the desert to Tunisia.

. . . and Marriage?

It was extremely difficult for a civilian to get a passage home to the UK during the war. Priority was given to people on health grounds or to those who were travelling on Government business. I fitted neither category, but hopefully put my name on the waiting list. This was held by the Manager of Thomas Cooks, who was one of the few people in the know about shipping movements.

At last, in the Autumn of 1944 I was given twenty-four hours' notice of my sailing on a troop ship. Of course, I wasn't ready, hadn't even got a trunk, let alone packed it. My father "had a word" with Thomas Cook's manager and, although I should have gone to the bottom of the waiting list, I was promised a place on the next available sailing.

I found a second-hand tin-lined officer's trunk at the club and was ready when the next summons came in February.

I had no compunction now about leaving home. I longed to be free of parental supervision and Joan was at last well enough to be left. Also I longed to get home to England. Six years in one place had made Egypt feel claustrophobic. By now I was tired of the relentless heat and dirt and flies and noise. And the growing feeling that I had never felt before, that the English were unwanted. England beckoned like some earthly paradise: a land of smiling meadows and London double-decker buses and friendly people. Also I was going to *get married,* although I hadn't thought through what this represented. We hadn't discussed how we were going to live or where. Desmond had no qualifications. Would we live in Liverpool or London or . . .? I had complete faith in Desmond's ability to solve these problems.

I didn't give much thought to what my leaving home meant to my parents. My father in particular may have felt bereft. We were still close in spite of his inability to discuss emotional matters and my refusal to discuss my future plans; and in spite of the heartache I must have caused him in the early years of the war. He stoically accepted my determination to go back to England. Joan probably by now would have missed me also, although she never said as much. She did write later and tell me that Abdul, our cook, had wept unrestrainedly after my departure. Abdul? He had been my father's cook for the previous ten years. He was part of the household, but he was only a servant. It never entered my feather-brain that he might have been fond of me and might miss me.

I am often asked 'What was it like living in Egypt?' My answer has to be 'It was home. I took it for granted.' I both loved and was exasperated by Egypt, just as an Englishman both loves and is exasperated by his country. I took this extraordinary country for granted.

I was the child of a broken family, relying on a support network of kind adults and fantastic friends and I had my personal experiences of the Second World War. These were the things I *felt* about. Egypt was the background to my growing up.

I took for granted the heat, the cacophony and the Babel of different languages being spoken in the streets, the flies, the beggars, the poverty; the gentleness and humour of the Egyptians, their unfailing courtesy and generosity; the wise-looking old men gazing into space as they puffed on their *nargilehs* (water pipes) while fingering their amber prayer beads or idly flicking their ornate fly whisks; the magnificent oriental opulence of Shepheard's and Mena House Hotels; the wide splendid spaces of the desert and the way its sands spilled down from the Pyramids towards Mena House, only to be arrested by the hotel gardens; the constant sound of birds singing, the cicadas making their ugly grinding sound outside the Sharia Fuad el Awal flat; the ethereal beauty of the jacaranda tree I could see from our drawing-room balcony, the scarlet flame of the forest trees, the palm trees and eucalyptus trees, the awe-inspiring banyan trees; the sound of the *muezzin*'s five-daily call to prayer and the sight of men kneeling on prayer mats in the street in response; the silent servants in their spotless white *galabiehs,* red cummerbunds and tarbooshes; clapping one's hands for service if one only needed a glass of water; the privileged enclave of the Club, itself within the privileged enclave of Gezira; the freedom of the swimming pool and the freedom from fear as one walked the streets, both as a small child and as an adolescent girl; lazily watching cricket at the club or dancing the night away; the petty snobberies and racism of some of the British at the club; the cut and thrust of fascinating conversations at our dining table when we had visitors; the wealth of fruit we ate: fresh figs and dates, mangoes, guavas and apricots as well as the more mundane apples, oranges and bananas; relaxing in the peaceful grounds of the Anglo-Egyptian Union; the astounding technicolour sunsets, the almost palpable silver moonlight; the meek donkeys and the supercilious camels making their slow way through the streets, their necks hung with blue beads to ward off the evil eye, it was said; the inefficiency of the Egyptian Civil Service and the unspoken need to bribe or "have a word"; and again the heat of the sun but also the coolness of the flats, with their stone or marble floors and shuttered windows; the delicious cool evening breeze; open air cinemas and the Parisiana, the Greek open-air restaurant where one could get a whole meal of *mezzes* for the price of a drink: one would see whole families at tables laden with olives and crisps and canapés, drinking only beer or *gasoozas* (fizzy lemonades). At the Parisiana also one could choose one's own steak (camel) to be cooked for dinner; the smells of garlic and spices or of the jasmine wreaths being touted in the Cairo streets at night; wandering through the narrow streets of the *Muski,* surrounded by brasses, silks, brocades and jewellery and bargaining good-naturedly with the shopkeeper over cups of thick sweet Turkish coffee; the clanging trams, overflowing in the centre with Arabs, at one end of the tram the more decorous First Class compartment and at the other end the *harem,* reserved for women. Mostly I remember the heat and the noise and the constant bustle of activity.

All this I had taken for granted and left behind carelessly. I couldn't wait to start a new life, in England, as an adult. Only later was I to realise how much I would miss it.

My parents had two distractions almost immediately after I had left. Firstly – and I was sad, a little guilty, to miss this – my father celebrated his fifty years as a journalist. He must have been sixty-eight, because he wrote his first regular pieces for the *Glasgow Herald* when he was eighteen. Then he wrote the Aberdeen theatre reviews while at the same time managing and occasionally appearing in a Music Hall. (He boasted that he had put Harry Lauder, then a coal miner, on the stage.) Apart from a short spell as a teacher in Alexandria and serving in the Artists' Rifles during the Great War, he had always worked as a journalist. Even during that war he was seconded to Intelligence to produce an Arabic newspaper for the Egyptian Labour Corps.

To celebrate this anniversary there was a collection towards a cheque amounting to £1,000 (more than a year's salary for him at the time) and a reception at the Embassy when Lord Killearn, representing the Ministry of Information, gave it to him, together with a scroll naming the donors. My father was most touched that the latter included not only the great and good of Cairo society, but also obscure people whom he had known in the distant past.

Also in honour of this anniversary he was awarded the Order of the Nile (Second Class), having been awarded the Fourth Class after the First World War, for services to Anglo-Egyptian relations. He was now in a position to call himself Philip Taylor Bey, but he never used the title. He was of course gratified by this, as he was both gratified and amused that this news made the front page of the *Daily Mail*. He had been its faithful correspondent for almost all of his fifty years as a journalist and was proud of it. (In these degenerate days I feel obliged to defend my father's pride in his long service of both the *Mail* and the *Telegraph*. In his day, the *Mail*, the first ever tabloid, was right wing as it is now, but it was also a respectable, responsible family newspaper. The *Telegraph* had a reputation for being the broadsheet that provided the widest coverage of hard news.)

The other distraction was that Vere Harmsworth, son of Lord Rothermere, proprietor of the *Daily Mail*, was posted to Cairo and lodged with my parents for some time. I think they really enjoyed having him.

My father saw me off at Cairo station, putting me in a carriage with an Englishwoman and her two small children bound for the same boat. Mrs. Morgan came from Bahrein, known then as a white man's graveyard, and was clearly going home on health grounds. She looked white and worn out and must have been dismayed at having been asked to keep an eye on me, particularly as I felt and must have looked miserable all the way to Alexandria. So much for freedom from one's parents!

When we got to Alex we weren't able to go aboard and were put up for the night in a hotel. While I was sitting forlornly in my hotel room, Mrs. Morgan came to invite me to go and have something to eat with her and the children in town. We went to Pastroudi's (I think) and had a delicious meal and on the way back to the hotel, in a *gharri*, clattering past the colourful, noisy crowds, I suddenly felt elated. I was free! My father wouldn't be waiting up for me, asking questions, as he had done for the past five years. It was the very beginning of my adulthood.

The next day we boarded our ship. It was a Liberty ship, one of a fleet built by the Americans. Before they entered the war, there were many ways in which the US helped the Allies and the building of Liberty ships was one of them. They were small cargo ships, built at great speed to replace the Merchant Navy ships which were being torpedoed at an unacceptable rate. (More than 1,000 ships by the end of 1940. This represented not only terrible loss of life, but also the attempted starving out of the UK.)

I was delayed going through Customs and when I at last went aboard, the First Mate was waiting for me at the top of the gangway. He looked at me in disbelief. 'Miss Taylor? You are very lucky!' I don't know what tale had been spun by Thomas Cooks to get me aboard, but I had been allocated the doctor's cabin, with bathroom en suite (everyone else shared four to a cabin). The First Mate had understood that Miss Taylor was an aged spinster, going home to lay her bones in England. Furthermore, I was given a place of honour on the left of the Captain; an elderly Naval Officer was on his right. The Captain was none too pleased to have this slip of a girl in the place of honour, but after a whispered consultation with the First Mate he accepted the situation and I was not removed below the salt. By the end of the voyage the Captain had taken a fatherly interest in me and even kissed me goodbye. I did before long give my cabin up to an importunate and rather neurotic woman and her ten-year-old son.

We were a motley company, about fifteen of us, mostly middle-aged. We read and talked and played cribbage in the evening.

Liberty ships were fast and it had been agreed that we should speed home, without the need of linking up with a convoy. But when we got to Gibraltar we had to stay in port for a couple of days. A German submarine was known to be lurking nearby and we had to wait until it was deemed safe to move on. The idea now was that we should after all join a convoy in the Atlantic where we would be slower, but protected by British warships. In the meantime, we had to move at full speed towards the convoy.

Eventually we sailed off and when we were out of sight of land we broke down. The ship floated on a still calm sea in full sunshine while we could hear the sounds of tinkering coming from the engines. The neurotic mother had hysterics. I felt absolutely calm, although there was every chance that a submarine was around. This was my third "brush with death". Eventually we moved on, this time straight out into the Atlantic in order to join a convoy.

This convoy, when we eventually came in sight of it, was extraordinarily impressive – like a floating city. As we got nearer we realised it was moving at a stately pace with destroyers darting round it like harassing sheepdogs. We slipped neatly into the row of ships allocated to us and were welcomed by hootings and passengers waving from the other ships.

We landed at Gourock and travelled on the night train from Glasgow to London. I began to experience culture shock. I hadn't expected the rudeness of the porter at Glasgow, nor the impatient rudeness of the telephone operator when I rang Mollie to tell her I was home. I was in the next few weeks to meet with more irritation and rudeness from petty bureaucrats. I suppose that by 1945 and after nearly six years of wartime shortages, tolerance and good manners were in short supply, but it came as a shock nevertheless. Fed up as I had been with Egypt, I had never met with anything but courtesy from the Egyptians. Cheating, sometimes, and stealing, sometimes, but always courtesy!

But it was wonderful to get off the train at Cookham Station to be greeted by Mollie and to drive through the still unspoilt and beautiful countryside to their home on the Thames.

The Clarks still lived in the two converted boathouses, to which they had evacuated after they were bombed out in Kent and now had two adopted children, Peter and Fiona, aged four and six respectively. Moored at the bottom of the lawn was Kathlamba, a large four-berthed boat which provided extra accommodation when they had an overspill. I was to love sleeping on Kathlamba, listening to the water gently lapping the boat. The boathouses were at the bottom of Winter Hill and the garden sloped steeply up the hill to the access road. A winding path had been made down the garden, but John had also built a strong but distinctly home-made lift powered by electricity.

At the top of the garden was tethered Jenny the goat, at the bottom near the boathouses there were chickens and rabbits and off the dry dock, fenced in from the main river, we had ducks. We had plentiful supplies of delicious eggs always, but Mollie never had the heart to eat the chickens and rabbits. There was the inevitable Irish setter, Judy (Mollie replaced each setter from the same kennels), a Bedlington and probably a couple of cats, though I don't remember them.

John's family firm which refined sugar for breweries had been evacuated from Millwall to Manchester and John was home only at weekends. He usually brought home goodies, some I suspect bought on the black market, some gifts from his Masonic friends. Tripe I remember best, which Mollie cooked in a delicious onion sauce.

It was my first real chance to get to know John and it wasn't long before I learned he had two passions, apart from home and family: boating and Kipling, which he was fond of quoting. He was a kind man who tolerated with good grace the many young people who, like me, were attracted to Mollie and treated Riverwood as their second home, His daughter by his first marriage, Jacqueline, known as Sprat, was a frequent visitor. She was about twelve at the time, at school at Berkhamstead, and spent most holidays at Cookham. Fiona soon acquired the nickname of Shrimp to be on equal terms with her adoptive sister.

Mollie had changed. She was still mischievous, warm and affectionate and had open house to all comers, but she was no longer the frivolous flirt. Her moods had become capricious, she was extremely judgmental and found it difficult to be crossed. She was now a pillar of the village community. She ran the Nursery Group at a small private school, Herries, in Cookham Dean and also ran a Guide company and Brownie pack. She and John had adopted Peter and Fiona after their father had been killed at the battle of Monte Cassino in Italy and they and their mother had been bombed out in London. Fiona had been injured and admitted to Great Ormond Street Hospital and Peter had been billeted on Mollie and John temporarily. It was then that the Clarks conceived the idea of adopting both brother and sister. They were a lively pair, in spite of the fact that Mollie was extremely strict with them. I used to wonder at this, because she had been almost careless in her discipline with her own daughters and me. It must have been part of her character change since the death of Jeannine and Romalita.

I arrived in March 1944 with the idea of spending a short while in Cookham and then moving to London and getting a job, perhaps in journalism. Desmond was still in France, taking part in the Battle of the Ardennes and it was uncertain when he would get home leave. However, Mollie and John had another plan. It was that I should stay with them, help Mollie in the Nursery Group and take it over in the Autumn, enabling her to give up the job. In the meantime, in preparation for my marriage, I could learn how to run a home and how to cook. By the time they suggested this, I had fallen completely in love with their lifestyle and the plan seemed to make good sense.

Life in the boathouses seemed to me perfection, after the sophisticated city life of Cairo. Everything had to be worked for, the living conditions were primitive, we had to plod from living quarters to bedrooms whatever the weather and to go out to a decrepit bathroom containing an Elsan lavatory. Once a week, John disgorged its contents, I don't like to think where. To get to school we climbed up the very, very steep slopes of Winter Hill in all weathers.

Each afternoon after school, we took the dinghy out with Jenny the goat and the two dogs, so that Jenny could find food on the nearby island and we could pick rabbit food. Petrol was rationed and although the allowance for country people was generous, the car was only used for essentials. I made the half-hour walk into church in Marlow each Sunday through Quarry Woods. To go to the pictures in Marlow, we rowed the dinghy across the river, tied it up to the root of a tree and walked through the fields. During the day Woottons, the boat builders next door, ran a ferry on demand across the river with one of their punts.

I thought to live like this forever would be bliss. The greatest miracle of all after Egypt was watching Spring unfold. We were on the edge of Quarry Woods and each day one watched the leaves of the beech trees unfurling. Each morning (no artificial insecticides) there would be new wild flowers growing up the side of the garden path until the hill was a riot of colour. I was enchanted by it all.

And I enjoyed helping Mollie in the Nursery Group each morning. In the afternoons I was allocated different jobs: taking mental arithmetic with Transition; reading Just So Stories to the children while they waited to go into dancing class; nature walks, though I hardly knew a daffodil from a bluebell or an oak from an ash. But the children enjoyed running wild and if they asked me a question I couldn't answer I looked it up with the intention of telling them later. At the end of the school day there was tea in the staff room with bread toasted on the electric fire. It was all very cosy. Herries School took boys of prep school age and girls to the age of sixteen. Private and very expensive, I was paid a pittance (£3 a week of which Mollie took £1 for my keep), but I was unqualified so it seemed fair, and I was happy. I joined the staff art class on a Monday evening and a small choir of ladies' voices. We gave recitals in private houses and must have worn hats for them, because I remember borrowing a highly unsuitable hat from Mollie which caused much amusement.

It was easy to get up to London by bus and train and I used to go and see my mother. She had been in London all through the war and had at one stage braved the nightly Blitz to go to night work. She lived in a bedsitter in Notting Hill Gate, not at that time fashionable, but it was central. She was fairly well pickled in alcoholism, but managed cleverly to conceal this from me and could talk intelligently and knowledgeably about world affairs and the arts. She could do this until she died, however poor and alcoholic, because she always read her *Daily Telegraph* and absorbed it. I once expressed surprise at this, as she was still very left-wing. 'You have to know what the enemy think' was her reply. But I suspect her incorrigible snobbery also had something to do with it. I enjoyed her company. She was entertaining and informed. But she could be my cruellest critic and because, as the analysts would say, I hadn't begun to resolve my relationship with her, she was to continue to have too strong an influence over me.

The flying bombs were still active, so it was quite an adventure to go up to London. I noticed how strained people were. Mollie sent me to see my mother on one occasion with a pie dish filled with wild flowers embedded in moss from the garden. I walked through Hyde Park to our usual meeting place at Marble Arch and noticed how greedily people's eyes followed the flowers. Hyde Park itself had been dug up to form a series of allotments, the railings removed to make armaments.

On one of my first visits to London the Clarks asked me to find a toy to give to Peter on his fourth birthday. Toys were not to be found in Maidenhead or Marlow. They gave me the name of a famous toyshop in Oxford Street. The shelves were pretty bare when I got there, but I did find a toy engine made of plain wood, varnished. Mollie and John were delighted and I hope Peter was.

Suddenly Desmond wrote to say he would be home on leave in May. The plan was that we would both spend a week with his family and a week at Cookham Dean.

His sister Sheila, who lived in London, and I travelled up together to Liverpool. It was a fairly silent journey, Sheila and I having little in common and both feeling shy. From then on the holiday took on the quality of a dream. Desmond's parents lived in a bungalow in Crosby, a suburb of Liverpool. His father was elderly, his mother a plump friendly housewife. They gave me a most warm welcome, though they must have had misgivings. Sheila's husband who had served in the

Middle East had spoken about spoilt girls who couldn't even boil an egg. The next day Desmond arrived. We sat up most of the night talking and it was very good to be with him again.

While we were in Crosby the war in Europe came to an end: VE Day, which we celebrated modestly but noisily. Desmond's family lived in a crescent with a small green at its core. We lit a bonfire that night and danced around it, singing. *"Mairsy dotes"*, I remember. The correct words were "Mares eat oats and does eat oats and little lambs eat ivy, kids'll eat ivy too. Won't you?" pronounced "Mairsy dotes and dozy dotes and little lamsitivy. Kidslitivy too. Wont you?" Silly, but we felt silly with relief.

The second week at Riverwood is more vivid in my memory. We went up to London, once to meet my mother, once to see *Arsenic and Old Lace.* We boated on the river. On one occasion I suggested a walk in Quarry Woods. I had fantasised romantically about such a walk, but after a few minutes Desmond asked if we could go back. 'I can't stand it,' he said. 'I keep thinking there's a German sniper behind every tree.' This was the one and only time he referred to the stress of warfare.

Reader, I did not marry him. If Desmond hadn't pressed me to marry him on his next leave, I suppose we might have done so in time. But I took fright. John Clark put his finger on it when he later said I hadn't been ready for marriage.

But there were several reasons that contributed to my decision. We had been separated for two years and in spite of the fact that our friendship held firm, we weren't so relaxed with one another. Also the question of religion had by no means been resolved. Desmond was an Anglican and he was prepared to agree to the Catholic Church's then demands that we shouldn't use artificial contraception and that any children should be brought up as Catholics. Unbelievably, these were not subjects that we had ever discussed in depth. A further blow came when my mother made it plain she didn't consider Desmond good enough for me. The small child in me succumbed to her judgement, even though it was in floods of tears. But also, secretly, scarcely acknowledged, I was enjoying my first freedom from family commitments.

(I was to see Desmond once more. Staying at Riverwood for a few days in the Fifties, John announced one evening that "a friend of mine" was coming for the weekend. This was Desmond, now working as a rep for a pharmaceutical company, married with a son of five, Stephen.

It was an emotional meeting and when he arrived we both reached instantly for a cigarette. The mutual attraction and friendship was still there and we had an uneasy couple of days in the constant presence of the Clarks.

Still later I had news of him. I was invited to a communal party on the evening of Prince Charles' and Di's wedding. The other couple in our party were a surgeon and his wife, both of whom I discovered came from Crosby. It then transpired, in an extraordinary coincidence, that the husband and Desmond had lived in the same street, both gone to Merchant Taylors and their mothers were close friends. The general reminded his wife that Desmond had been at their wedding: "a real card!" He then told me that, sadly, Desmond had died quite young of some rare disease.)

One day, standing in the kitchen, I saw through the window Mollie's brother Gerry hurtling down the garden path. After five years as a prisoner of war, first in Germany, then in Poland, he had been released on VE Day and had made a tortuous journey through Europe to get home, He had determined to come back unannounced and when Mollie, who was gardening, saw him she threw herself into his arms. I went out. 'And Pete too!' said Gerry and enveloped us both in an enormous bear hug. What a moment! He stayed at Riverwood several weeks before being demobbed. We talked and talked. It was so good to have him back with the family, little changed, a bit more serious.

I paid a short visit to the Llewellyns at the start of the summer holidays. Aunt Rosie and Jane were now living in Broadstone, Dorset, and Jane was attending day school in Bournemouth. Peggy was there, pregnant with her first child, Avril, and it was good again to be in the midst of the high-spirited Llewellyns. Donald was still serving with the RAF somewhere in England.

I had decided by then that I would train as a teacher. Judging by Herries it would be an enjoyable and easy way to earn a living, with lovely long holidays. That would suit me down to the ground!

My parents remained in Egypt, coming home for summer leave once the war was over. They left after the anti-British riots of the Fifties and after (ominously) a black cross was painted on their front door. They were allowed to take out only a few possessions and no money, relying on my father's savings in England over the years.

My mother worked for a while longer and when she retired developed a lifestyle unique to her: living in an interminable series of bedsitters, in London in the winter, in Brighton in the summer.

It wasn't long before I woke up to the fact that she was an incurable alcoholic and, after a period of angry bewilderment, I began to feel extreme pity for her: such a waste of a sensitive, intelligent and talented woman. She died in her beloved Brighton in 1963.

In August 1945 the Allies dropped an atomic bomb on Hiroshima. A week later the Japanese surrendered and the Second World War was over.

I resolved that these memoirs would finish with the end of the war and, as there are no neat endings in life . . .

THE END

Except that there is a Sequel . . .

SEQUEL

It only remains for me to reveal the Big Secret that was kept from me as a child and that I was never meant to know. I stumbled across it when I was thirty.

I wanted to go sailing off the south of France with a friend, but my passport had expired. I had had my own passport since the age of eleven when I had first travelled alone on one of the "children's boats", so anticipated no difficulty. However, a new regulation had been introduced. As I had been born in Dublin only months after Irish independence, I was not by birth a British subject and so had to produce my father's birth certificate.

That weekend I went home (my parents by now were living in England) and asked my father for his birth certificate.

This was not possible, he replied. He hadn't got it. I offered to go to Somerset House to get a copy. No, this was not possible either. 'Daddy,' I protested, 'I don't mind if you were illegitimate. I can easily get a copy.' No, this would not be possible.

That evening he and I went to the Savage Club for a Ladies' Night drinks party. We were joined by a poet friend, John Waller, and I enlisted John's help in persuading my father – which he tried to do. My father looked thoughtful, pursed his lips, shook his head and changed the subject.

Next morning my father felt unwell and stayed in bed. Joan, while choosing not to enlighten me herself, forbade me to raise the subject with him again as it might bring on a heart attack. I was still the dutiful daughter and complied with this request. I was irritated, but the last thing I wanted to do was to bring on a heart attack. My father had heart trouble and had already had one stroke.

My older cousins Beatie and David were visiting that weekend. 'He's gone to bed and won't speak to me,' I complained. 'All I want is his birth certificate.'

Beatie then told me what was behind this extraordinary behaviour. It's a long but interesting story, and this is what I pieced together from what she and my mother subsequently told me.

My grandmother, Christina Grant, like so many lively young Victorian women, went off to the Middle East in search of adventure. She got a job as a governess in Beirut which at that time was a sophisticated and westernised city, known as the Paris of the Middle East. There she fell in love with and married a Lebanese. All I know about him is that he was comfortably off (balls in the garden were mentioned by Beatie) and a Maronite Christian. The Maronites were members of the early Eastern Orthodox Church, who united with the Roman church at the time of the Crusades. Educated and influenced by French Jesuits in the nineteenth century, they were emerging as the most powerful group in Lebanese society. Tina converted to Catholicism in order to marry and she and her husband had two sons, my father Philip, and his younger brother Charlie.

In 1882, when they were four and two respectively, Tina's husband died and she brought her two sons home to Aberdeen to educate them and bring them up as Scots boys. She earned her living as a teacher of French and the piano and in due course married Joseph Taylor, who, either then or later, worked in the National Bank of Egypt and was a composer of popular music. At least one song was published: *The Empire Waltz,* of which I have a copy.

For many years Tina kept in touch with her family in Beirut and when my cousin Beatie was a young girl, nearly forty years later, a Salamoni cousin Neville (?) visited Aberdeen. He wanted to marry her but nice though he was and in spite of the "lovely" letters he wrote to her afterwards, the young couple did not marry. Beatie couldn't enlighten me any more about the family and Tina had rarely spoken about her early married life, so there is a maddening blank in this story.

When my father left school, he first managed a music hall in Aberdeen, as well as appearing in some of the sketches. He also dabbled in journalism, writing Aberdeen theatre reviews for the *Glasgow Daily Herald.* As a matter of interest, he used to claim that he was the first to promote advertising by post.

But my father's heart was in journalism.

When he was in his twenties, my father joined his mother and stepfather in Alexandria. There, Tina was working again as a governess, this time to two young princesses, Princesses Haliak and Aliah. My father got a job teaching in a Catholic school.

A job became available as sub-editor of *The Egyptian Gazette,* an English daily then produced in Alexandria, and my father wanted to apply for it. When he consulted one of the priests at his school, the latter advised him to change his name to that of his stepfather: Taylor. He would never make his way in Alexandrian society with the surname of Salamoni. He was virtually a Scot, spoke like one, had been educated in Aberdeen, and could pass himself off easily as British. My father followed this advice, got the job and professionally never looked back.

It may seem extraordinary these days that he did this, but I have mentioned before the mindset of the British at the turn of the century. It was class-ridden and racist. This was brought all the more home to me recently when I read *The Map of Love.* In this novel Ahdaf Souief describes how a young English girl of good birth at the start of the twentieth century goes to Egypt and marries an Egyptian, also of good birth. As a result she is shunned by all her English friends, including those at the British Embassy, apart from the Anglican Dean's wife. I can believe it. The novel is set in 1901, about the time my grandmother and father went out to Alexandria.

By the time I was born some twenty years later, the deception was complete. Philip had become a successful journalist, a respected member of the British community (Caledonian Club, secretary of The British Union, Rotarian, etc.), had served as an officer in the Artists' Rifles and Intelligence during the Great War and been Mentioned in Despatches. There was no going back for him and how could he have explained any of this to a child? I now also realise he didn't want it to be known that he had a Lebanese father because my chances in Cairo society would be effected. (By the time I was a teenager this had become less and less true, but he couldn't have known that.) It amazes me now that I never once asked questions about my paternal grandfather. Perhaps it was because I was young and the young are so busy living in the present that they care little about the past.

I was shocked when I was told the truth of the matter and must have felt much as an adopted child feels when they are told the truth in adulthood. I was the same person as the day before, and yet I was somebody quite different. I was also angry with my father for deceiving me for so long.

It is with sadness that I record that I didn't fully forgive him before his death five years after this incident. Now, fifty years on, I completely understand why he acted as he did. He will not have been alone! I met in Egypt and still meet in this country people whom I recognise as possibly having mixed blood without realising it. One of their ancestors will have acted as did my father and of course many Jews have had completely to assume the characteristics of their adopted country in fear of persecution or prejudice.

It seems such a small matter in these days of open inter-marriage, but it was not so a hundred years ago, or even fifty years ago. All the assumptions that I had made throughout my thirty years about my family and myself – about what it was to be a British child of Empire – all these assumptions had to be re-absorbed and altered. It has been an interesting inner journey!

P.O. 2004

Acknowledgements

Artemis Cooper.   *Cairo in the War 1939-45.* Hamish Hamilton.

Anwar el-Sadat.   *In Search of Identity.* Fontana/Collins.

C.S. Jarvis.   *Oriental Spotlight.* John Murray.

Sr. M. Gregory Kirkus. *Mary Ward: A Woman's Courage in Adversity.*

Penelope Lively.   *A House Unlocked.* Penguin/Viking.

Gerald O'Farrell.   *The Tutankhamun Deception.* Sidgwick and Jackson.

Christopher Pick.   *Egypt. A Traveller's Anthology.* John Murray.

Ahdaf Soueif.   *The Map of Love.* Bloomsbury.

Anon   *A Will to do Well.* St. Mary's School, Cambridge.

Further Reading

Lawrence Durrell.   *The Alexandria Quartet.* Faber and Faber.

Robert Graves.   *Goodbye to All That.* Jonathan Cape.

Penelope Lively.   *Moon Tiger.* André Deutsch.
     Oleander, Jacaranda. Viking.

Naguib Mahfouz. ＊ ~~*The Levant Trilogy.* Penguin.~~

Countess of Ranfurly. *To War with Whitaker.* Mandarin.

Olivia Manning.   *The Levant Trilogy.* Penguin

＊ *The Cairo Quartet* Doubleday